REBEL KERRY

⁓ FROM THE PAGES OF *THE KERRYMAN* ⁓

EDITED BY SIMON BROUDER

MERCIER PRESS

Irish Publisher – Irish Story

MERCIER PRESS

Cork

www.mercierpress.ie

© *The Kerryman*, 2017

ISBN: 978 1 78117 478 4

10 9 8 7 6 5 4 3 2 1

A CIP record for this title is available from the British Library

Images on pp. 20–1 (the *Castro/Aud*) and 128–9 (British military at Ballymullen Barracks, Tralee) courtesy of Mercier Press.

Printed and bound in the EU.

CONTENTS

ACKNOWLEDGEMENTS

The Kerryman would like to thank the following for their contributions to this book:

Ryle Dwyer, historian and journalist, who has written several books, notably on the period from 1916 to the Civil War, such as *Tans, Terror and Troubles: Kerry's Real Fighting Story 1913–23*.

Hélène O'Keeffe, author of *To Speak of Easter Week*, who has profiled several key figures from the era. Hélène had recourse to the Irish Life and Lore Oral History collection – the oral history recordings established by her historian parents, Maurice and Jane O'Keeffe – in researching the testimony of relatives of the 1916 generation.

The RTÉ Archives, for permission to reproduce Captain Ó Lochlainn's account of the Ballykissane incident in Dónal Nolan's 'Captain Ó Lochlainn: The Man in Charge during Ballykissane'.

Kerry County Librarian and Archivist Michael Lynch, who has been a vital source of information and support in the search for 1916 materials.

Thanks also to *The Kerryman* contributors and designers: Tommy King, Dónal Nolan, Kevin Hughes, Brian Ó Conchubhair and Amy Reidy.

Editor's Note

This book is based on three supplements produced by *The Kerryman* to mark the centenary of the Easter Rising. It comprises a carefully selected sample of contemporary articles from the paper, archive photographs and new research by leading historians and *The Kerryman*'s own staff, exploring the events that occurred in Kerry between 1916 and 1923. Unfortunately, for reasons set out in the introduction, there are no contemporary articles from *The Kerryman* in the Civil War period as the paper was not printed for the duration of that conflict.

ABBREVIATIONS

BMH	Bureau of Military History
CPS	Crown Prosecution Service
CWS	Co-operative Wholesale Society
DMP	Dublin Metropolitan Police
DORA	Defence of the Realm Act
DSO	Distinguished Service Order
GAA	Gaelic Athletic Association
GPO	General Post Office
IPP	Irish Parliamentary Party
IRA	Irish Republican Army
IRB	Irish Republican Brotherhood
IVF	Irish Volunteer Force
KC	King's Counsel
LLD	Doctor of Laws
MCC	Member of County Council
MP	Member of Parliament
NCO	Non-Commissioned Officer
NUI	National University of Ireland
OP	Ordo Praedicatorum (the Dominicans)
RDC	Rural District Council
RIC	Royal Irish Constabulary
TD	Teachta Dála
WS	Witness Statement

INTRODUCTION

THE KERRYMAN AND THE FIGHT FOR INDEPENDENCE

Simon Brouder

COSTING just one penny, very good value at the time, and backed by an investment of £500, the first edition of *The Kerryman* landed on news stands in Kerry on 27 August 1904. Though many predicted that *The Kerryman* would not stand the test of time, the paper set up by cousins Tom and Daniel Nolan and Maurice Griffin is still bringing the news to the people of Kerry over a century later. Nevertheless the paper did have its share of difficulties, particularly in its turbulent early years. Some of *The Kerryman*'s most severe tests came following the Easter Rising and during the War of Independence, when it found itself

Kerryman **staff outside the paper's original offices on Edward Street, Tralee, c. 1910.**

at the very heart of the independence struggle in Kerry. Founded on staunch republican grounds, *The Kerryman* was, on several occasions, in direct conflict with crown forces.

In *The Kerryman's* early years the Nolans and Griffin sought readers among the followers of the Gaelic Athletic Association (GAA), the Gaelic League and Arthur Griffith's Sinn Féin, rather than adherents of the pervasive Home Rule and Irish Parliamentary Party (IPP) movements. Both of the latter movements held great sway over public opinion in Kerry and their view, that Irish independence could best be won by currying the favour of the British establishment, was the dominant one of the day.

However, it was not an opinion shared by *The Kerryman* and its sister evening paper *The Liberator*. By the time the Rising was about to erupt on the streets of Dublin, the two papers had firmly drawn a stridently republican line in the sand. *The Kerryman's* editorial position at first attracted only a relatively small cohort of readers – in the early years the print run averaged about 1,300 copies a week – but as both the Gaelic and independence movements grew in popularity, more readers in Kerry came to share *The Kerryman's* way of thinking. As a result, by the time the Rising took place, and in the months that followed, *The Kerryman's* anti-imperial stance had earned it an influential position in the county.

The general unwillingness of *The Kerryman* to back the British war effort, and its resistance to aiding army recruitment, had already fostered a frosty, if not positively icy, relationship between the paper and the British establishment. That Kerry's most ardently republican paper had become one of the county's most read and most powerful titles was anathema to crown forces and they did the paper and its staff few favours. It was against this backdrop that *The Kerryman* had the first of its major showdowns with the forces of the British Empire.

In the immediate wake of the Rising the Royal Irish Constabulary (RIC) and British troops cut a swathe across Kerry, arresting around sixty suspected rebels and sympathisers in a matter of days. As well as co-founding *The Kerryman*, Maurice Griffin had helped establish a branch of Sinn Féin in the county. As a result he was a prime target for the British, who, quite wrongly, blamed Sinn Féin for instigating the insurrection. On Tuesday 9 May 1916, just ten days after Patrick Pearse's surrender in Dublin and following the executions of twelve rebel leaders, soldiers swept into *The Kerryman*'s Tralee printworks on Edward Street, above which Griffin lived, to arrest him. Within seconds of the army's arrival he was unceremoniously dragged from his room and hauled out past the presses and into the yard. There, he was pinned against the wall and interrogated by British troops as the paper's nervous but defiant staff looked on. During this questioning the British officer in charge told Griffin, in no uncertain terms, that should there be any attempt to rescue him the soldiers were under orders to shoot him dead on the spot.

Griffin was then spirited away, along with eighteen other Tralee men who had been lifted by the British, and placed in a cell at Tralee's Ballymullen Barracks. He spent six days imprisoned in Tralee before he was transported to Richmond Barracks in Dublin, ahead of an eventual move to Wakefield Prison in West Yorkshire. His incarceration in Wakefield was brief. He arrived at the prison on 23 May and was released just six days later, on 29 May, when he was put on a boat back to Dublin.

His release was, obviously, front-page news in *The Kerryman*, which carried an interview with Griffin about his brief prison experience in its 3 June edition. He was remarkably unperturbed about his short time in jail, saying that he 'would not have liked to have missed the experience of prison life'.

British troops once again invaded *The Kerryman*'s offices just a few months after Griffin's release. This time it was the paper itself they targeted, though the raid was once more linked to Griffin. The reason for the raid was a letter published in *The Liberator* on 19 August from Henry Brassil, a Tralee native living in London. In his letter Brassil had congratulated Griffin on his release and suggested that 'a campaign of agitation' be launched, calling for the release of Austin Stack, commandant of the Kerry Brigade, and other men who had been 'unconstitutionally convicted'.

This letter incensed the British authorities. When a copy of the paper landed on the Dublin Castle desk of the head of British forces in Ireland, General Sir John Maxwell, he immediately ordered that *The Kerryman* and *The Liberator* be shut down and all the papers' equipment seized. In early September a large force of British soldiers and RIC officers sealed off Edward Street and the adjacent Castle Street and descended on the offices of the two papers. Inside the printworks, a company of army engineers set about dismantling the presses, a task they actually carried out with great care, packing all the equipment into crates, which were then carried off to Ballymullen Barracks. Once the work was complete, and in front of a large crowd who had gathered to watch the commotion, General Maxwell's order was nailed to the door of the print works by RIC Inspector Hill. The order stated that the presses had been shut down and seized as a result of 'a certain matter the publication of which was calculated to cause disaffection'. This was the first time one of Maxwell's repression orders, issued under the Defence of the Realm Act (DORA), was aimed at an Irish newspaper. It would not be the last.

However, the Nolans, Griffin and *The Kerryman* staff were not about to let the British Empire get in the way of delivering the news. They arranged to have shortened editions of *The Kerryman* printed by The Gaelic Press in Dublin and these were then smuggled into Kerry and into the hands of an eager readership by friendly railway workers. After a few weeks the British realised the futility of their action and Maxwell's order was rescinded. The printing equipment was returned, in perfect condition, and *The Kerryman* and *The Liberator* resumed printing in Tralee on 30 September 1916.

The Kerryman was again suppressed briefly in 1919, along with many other Irish papers, after it printed advertising for the sale of bonds to support Dáil Éireann. Though equipment wasn't seized this time, the paper was prevented from printing for several weeks in February and March and again in July and August.

The paper once again fell victim to the British in November 1920, during the so-called 'Siege of Tralee', when the Black and Tans imposed a reign of terror on the town and its people. The Tans' brutal ten-day campaign led to mass starvation, as they prevented food deliveries into the town, and saw at least eight people killed and numerous businesses burned. It also meant *The Kerryman* could not be printed for a fortnight.

When the paper eventually returned, it did so in characteristically defiant fashion. Rather than dwell on the Tans' brutality, *The Kerryman* was determined to move on. The only comment on the matter was brief and to the point: 'We do not deem it necessary to dilate on the situation which compelled us to shut down our business for two weeks,' the editor wrote.

While *The Kerryman* emerged largely unscathed from its initial encounters with the British forces, the next showdown proved to be far more punishing. A few weeks after the 'siege' ended, a new British officer, Major John Alastair MacKinnon, arrived in Tralee to take charge of the local Auxiliaries, which was the name of the paramilitary unit of the RIC. MacKinnon was a brutal enforcer of British imperial will and his time in Tralee saw numerous atrocities committed. The action that generated the most hostility against him came on Christmas Day 1920, when MacKinnon personally executed two young Irish Republican Army (IRA) men, John Leen and Maurice Reidy, in cold blood following a raid in Ballydwyer.

From then on MacKinnon was a marked man and the primary target of the Kerry IRA. It took the IRA, who set up a ten-man team to track the officer, four months to get to him. On 15 April 1921 he was shot dead by the IRA's Boherbee column while playing golf at Oakpark golf course. After the assassination the Auxiliaries descended on *The Kerryman*'s offices to demand that the evening's edition of *The Liberator* be printed with a heavy black border. Such borders were a newspaper tradition at the time, employed to mourn the passing of great figures. However, the staff of *The Kerryman* did not regard MacKinnon as a 'great figure' and they refused to comply, opting not to print at all rather than kowtow to British demands.

MacKinnon's death triggered an orgy of retaliation by the Auxiliaries, who went on a rampage in Tralee, burning numerous houses and businesses to the ground on the night of his funeral. *The Kerryman* was one of their main targets. A group of Auxiliaries stormed the print works and planted and detonated explosives, destroying the paper's presses. The little equipment that was left was finished off with sledgehammers and axes. *The Kerryman* and *The Liberator* remained out of print for the remainder of the War of Independence, finally returning in July 1923, just weeks after the end of the Civil War.

As a postscript it should be noted that the British armed forces were not the only ones to try to shut down *The Kerryman*. Decades later, at the height of the Troubles, the Provisional IRA also tried to muzzle the paper, and also failed. In one of the most notorious episodes in the history of *The Kerryman*, the IRA in 1974 threatened to murder then editor of the paper Seamus McConville. Just an hour into his first day as editor, McConville received an anonymous phone call warning him that he 'should make his last confession' if *The Kerryman* published an article by the late Con Houlihan. Houlihan's article was highly critical of the IRA and its efforts to repatriate the hunger-striking Price sisters from prison in Britain. Gardaí and an IRA contact told McConville and his staff that the threat was genuine and a cause for serious concern.

Like the Nolans and Griffin before him, McConville would not be intimidated. Determined to preserve the integrity of *The Kerryman*, he did not bow to the pressure from the IRA. The paper was printed and released as planned. That week every single *Kerryman* delivery van had a garda escort, and McConville's home was protected by gardaí for an entire month. During what was a frightening time for everyone at the paper, one IRA member arrived at *The Kerryman*'s offices with the explosive material gelignite, intending to blow up the building. Thankfully, as it was a church holiday, the building was closed and empty, so the would-be bomber left the scene.

In its long history *The Kerryman* has never allowed itself to be intimidated and has continued, week in week out, to deliver the news without fear or favour. It is a tradition we remain enormously proud of to this day.

ARRESTS THROUGHOUT KERRY

Saturday 13 May 1916

MANY PROMINENT MEN TAKEN INTO CUSTODY

TRALEE Tuesday.

Wholesale arrests of prominent members of the Irish Volunteer organisation are being effected throughout Kerry to-day.

IN TRALEE cavalry, infantry, and police turned out and halted opposite each house where arrests were made. Excitement ran high, but beyond the arrests nothing has to be recorded. Prominent amongst those arrested are:–

Mr. Maurice Griffin, part proprietor of the 'Kerryman' and 'Liberator'.
Mr. John P. O'Donnell, M.C.C.
Mr. P. J. Cahill, Secretary to a local firm of merchants.
Mr. Thomas Slattery, R.D.C.
Mr. P. J. Hogan, publican.
Mr. T. J. McCarthy, Engineer and Surveyor to R.D.C.
Mr. E. Barry, employee C.W.S.
Mr. Michael Doyle, carriage carpenter.
Mr. Daniel Healy, timekeeper.
Mr. Dan Finn, Urban Council steward.
Mr. William Farmer, labourer.

In outlying districts several arrests were also made, including the following from Castleisland:–

Mr. Bryan O'Connor, R.D.C., Gortgloss.
Mr. T. T. O'Connor, Cordal.
Mr. T Fitzgerald, publican, Castleisland.

THE RISING
IN KERRY

THE RISING'S FIRST CASUALTIES IN BALLYKISSANE

Dónal Nolan

IT was a young Killorglin woman who was inadvertently responsible for the first deaths of the Rising. History has it that the directions she innocently offered a group of men in a Briscoe touring car at the roadside in Killorglin ensured the name Ballykissane achieved a dark charge, alongside Banna, in the annals of Rising lore.

The Irish Volunteers' best-laid plans unravelled fast in the Kingdom, even before the first shot was fired in Dublin, making Kerry's role in the revolution significant and disastrous. Kerry had the dubious distinction of providing the first, watery, graves of the conflict, when the car driven by Limerick City Volunteer Thomas McInerney, with passengers Con Keating (Cahersiveen), Donal Sheehan (Monagea) and Belfast native Charlie Monaghan, made its fateful plunge from the pier in Ballykissane. News of the disaster, alongside the arrests of Roger Casement and Austin Stack a few miles north, hit the Rising effort hard in Munster in the subsequent days.

The occupants of the car had been on their way to a radio training school in Cahersiveen, where, along with mission leader Colm Ó Lochlainn and Cahersiveen man Denis Daly – travelling in a car ahead of them – they were to dismantle and steal vital radio equipment. It was part of Irish Republican Brotherhood (IRB) Supreme Council member Seán Mac Diarmada's plan to get radio equipment to Stack in Tralee. This would allow the Volunteers to establish communications with the *Aud* (originally called the *Castro*) in order to make arrangements to land at Fenit the 20,000 rifles and ten machine guns it was bringing from Germany.

The pier at Ballykissane, Killorglin, which Tom McInerney drove off on the night of 21 April 1916 during a mission to steal radio equipment in order to contact the *Aud*. Three of McInerney's fellow Volunteers drowned in the accident: Con Keating, Donal Sheehan and Charlie Monaghan. McInerney was the sole survivor. (Courtesy of Mercier Press)

Denis Daly, a close personal friend of Michael Collins from their time in the postal service in London together, stated to the Bureau of Military History (BMH) that it had been planned to erect the stolen radio in Ballyard, Tralee, from where the Volunteers were to try to contact the *Aud*. Tragically, we now know that the *Aud* did not have radio capability, making the whole Ballykissane misadventure a doomed one from the very start.

Daly, who had been a member of the IRB since 1913, also said there were plans to use the captured radio equipment to send 'misleading wireless messages' to units of the British navy to divert them from the Tralee Bay area while the arms were being landed. 'If true, this would pre-suppose that the British Admiralty code was in the possession of some member of our party. I did not have it, but, of course, Con Keating, as the wireless operator, would be the person most likely to have it,' Daly stated. There is also a suggestion that Donal Sheehan might have had the codes, having worked at the British War Office previously.

The whole doomed episode began on Good Friday morning, 21 April 1916, in Dublin, when Ó Lochlainn, Keating, Sheehan, Daly and Monaghan set off on the Killarney train under orders from Mac Diarmada to get the radio. Michael Collins handled the logistics at the Dublin end, meeting Ó Lochlainn at O'Connell Bridge to ensure he and his fellow Volunteers made the train. As captain on the special staff of Joseph Plunkett, Ó Lochlainn was in charge of the mission to Cahersiveen (although Daly later suggested that he was the leader). In his later recollections to the BMH, Ó Lochlainn recounted how the orders were 'clear enough':

> [G]et to Killarney, meet two Limerick cars there, swap code words with the chauffeurs, make for Caherciveen, enter Wireless School … dismantle transmitters and receivers, remove two portable sets … sprinkle petrol around, light up and light out for Tralee.

The five arrived in Killarney at about 7.30 p.m. on Good Friday. Daly recalled what happened next: 'On arrival in Killarney the five of us went to Charlie Foley's in New Street, where we had a meal. At the appointed time we went to the road junction outside the town where we were to meet the cars. The cars were there.'

The cars had been sent from Limerick, with McInerney behind the wheel of the brand-new Briscoe (the car that carried Keating, Sheehan and Monaghan as passengers) and Samuel Windrim behind the wheel of the other car, a Maxwell. As in all such missions, code words were required. In his deposition to the BMH, Clare native John J. Quilty – who owned the Briscoe, which he would have been driving himself but for a family emergency – recalled that the drivers were to ask the five Volunteers, 'Are you from Michael?' and for the reply the Volunteers were to say, 'Yes. Who are you? Are you from William?' It can only be presumed the words were exchanged faithfully on both sides, with little further time spent in Killarney before the two cars set out for Killorglin.

Ó Lochlainn and Daly rode in the lead car, checking regularly behind – according to Ó Lochlainn's later accounts – for their tail. 'I remember looking back every few minutes and seeing the headlights of the other car gleaming on the road or flashing in the sky as it topped a rise.'

As Daly was well known to the RIC in his home area, neither he nor Ó Lochlainn lingered on their way through Killorglin, anxious to avoid the police or 'bobbies'. However, they had no choice but to pull in when it became clear they had lost their comrades somewhere in the vicinity of Killorglin. Daly suspected afterwards that McInerney had ended up somehow driving on the Beaufort road, which would have led him in a straight path directly towards the pier at Ballykissane.

Whatever the reason for the mix-up in directions, McInerney stopped on the outskirts of Killorglin to ask a young girl for directions towards Cahersiveen. 'Take the first turn on the right' was her response. Some accounts have it that Keating, the one local man in the car, who would have known exactly how to get to his home town, was fast asleep in the back seat at the time of all the confusion. If so, it can only be assumed McInerney did not wish to bring any attention to his faulty navigating by waking Keating. He followed the directions, driving northwards towards Castlemaine harbour in the dead of night.

Like something from the silver screen, McInerney found the Briscoe suddenly teetering over the edge of the pier at Ballykissane. One long-held theory of many living in the area is that the smooth-flowing waters of the River Laune under moonlight and the lights from homes on the opposite bank might have combined to give the impression of a continuing roadway over the waters. The car's front wheels submerged in the water and it plunged into the deep and wide river within seconds.

**The wreckage of the Briscoe touring car retrieved from the
River Laune following the accident. (Courtesy of Mercier Press)**

McInerney was the only survivor of the disaster, managing to extricate himself from the car. Keating, Sheehan and Monaghan were likely trapped in their seats as the car went under, making the first casualties of the Rising particularly gruesome. The driver might well have drowned too, but for the intervention of local man Thady O'Sullivan, who came on the scene. McInerney had been swimming, disoriented, in the wrong direction, until O'Sullivan called out to guide him safely to shore.

Local man Patrick Begley and his son Michael were also on the scene and made strenuous efforts to rescue the Volunteers from the strong waters. They brought the despairing McInerney back to O'Sullivan's home and, after he had dried and warmed up, advised him to report the incident at the local RIC barracks. He reluctantly agreed and went to the barracks. It was when they picked up his wet overcoat while he was away that they discovered his revolver. This confirmed for them the furtive nature of McInerney's strange night-time jaunt.

Patrick Begley proved his bravery once more that night, when he hid the revolver by sitting on it under a cushion when the RIC arrived at O'Sullivan's house. The Kerry constables had been alerted to the Fenian activities by this point, with Casement and Stack already under arrest in Tralee.

The following morning – a wet Holy Saturday – fishermen recovered Keating and Sheehan's bodies, but Monaghan's remains were not found for another six months. McInerney meanwhile tried to recover his revolver on Holy Saturday morning, but the canny Patrick Begley advised him against carrying it for fear the RIC would return and find it on him. The police did return, as predicted, and arrested McInerney, who was transferred to Frongoch Internment Camp in Wales, along with the majority of those who were incarcerated, after the Rising. The Limerick man rejoined the IRA on his release from Frongoch and was later killed in an accidental shooting in Tipperary in 1922.

While obviously unaware of their comrades' fate, Daly and Ó Lochlainn soon realised the mission was doomed. They managed to get past an RIC checkpoint near Cahersiveen with a cover story about being medical students on their way to Waterville. Daly told the BMH that they knocked the mission on the head when it became clear to them that they were not going to be joined by the only member of the team with any radio expertise (i.e. Keating). However, Ó Lochlainn recalled that the RIC officers let it slip that security had been stepped up on the roads and around the wireless school, and suggested it was this fact that caused them to give up on the plan.

Whatever the reason, they made for the mountains, driving high into the Ballaghisheen Pass, where, according to Ó Lochlainn, they slept the night huddled together for warmth. Daly did not remember this detail, saying instead in his BMH statement that they drove straight for Killarney until the car broke down on the outskirts of the tourist town. Whatever happened, the pair made the Holy Saturday morning train to Dublin. Daly stated:

When changing trains at Mallow Station we met Mick Lynch, a brother of Diarmuid's, who told us that a man had been arrested and he believed he was Roger Casement. On Saturday night we brought the bag of tools [which Ó Lochlainn suggested they had ditched] to 44, Mountjoy Street and reported to Seán Mac Diarmada and Michael Collins. They were then aware of Casement's arrest.

Daly learned of his fellow Volunteers' fate in the Easter Sunday edition of the *Sunday Independent*. As he concludes in his BMH statement: 'My opinion still is that they took the Beaufort road on Good Friday night, thus losing contact with us in the first car, and coming into Killorglin on a road that went along directly to Ballykissane Pier.'

CAPTAIN Ó LOCHLAINN: THE MAN IN CHARGE DURING BALLYKISSANE

Dónal Nolan

CAPTAIN Colm Ó Lochlainn was the man in charge of the mission to steal the radio equipment from the wireless training school in Cahersiveen on Good Friday 1916. The following account of the episode, as recounted by Ó Lochlainn, is taken from the RTÉ Archives:

About 7.30 p.m. that April evening two motorcars stood outside Killarney station awaiting five of us who stepped off the Dublin train. Over goes Con Keating and the rest of us walked quietly through the town, the cars overtaking us at the college. Dinny Daly and myself took the first and away we went along the Killorglin road, the other following us about quarter of a mile astern.

According to a map – I still have it – the journey must have been about fourteen miles but I remember little of it, just the Kerry landscape slipping past: trees, hedgerows, grey stone walls with white gateposts here and there and the cool twilight deepening into night.

I remember looking back every few minutes and seeing the headlights of the other car gleaming on the road or flashing in the sky as it topped a rise.

I remember little of the journey because my mind was still filled with the excitement of a very full day.

Good Friday it was, in the year of glory 1916, and I had made an early start. As I jumped off my old Lucania at O'Connell Bridge, Michael Collins stepped out from the path. 'Here,' says Mick, 'I'll take the bike, you have your tickets, you have your orders, there's the tram.' I asked for that old bike later and Mick said it finished up in a barricade on Abbey Street corner.

There were five of us in the party. I was in charge, a captain on the special staff of Joe Plunkett, director of intelligence. Orders were clear enough: get to Killarney, meet two Limerick cars there, swap code words with the drivers, make for Cahersiveen, enter wireless school – said to be unguarded by the way – dismantle transmitters and receivers, remove two portable sets – Con Keating knew all about them – sprinkle petrol around, light up and light out for Tralee.

Austin Stack would meet us there at five in the morning with a farm cart to get one set. We were to go back to Limerick … board an early train at Long Pavement and take the second set to Athenry.

'Give it to George,' said Seán MacDermott, 'the boots at the hotel, he's alright, he's a member of the organisation and then get back to Dublin any way ye can.'

Such were my thoughts as the walls and hedgerows slipped past in the Kerry haze. And then we ran into the town of Killorglin and I saw no more flashes during that night … three miles or more we must have gone before I missed them.

We hurried through Killorglin; it wasn't a healthy place for Dinny, the RIC knew him too well. Now we slowed down hoping every moment to see the other car turn the corner, sometimes climbing, sometimes coasting downhill, always with eyes straining through the darkness for the following flash that never came.

Near Mountain Stage station we stopped at last and waited for over an hour and then decided that tyre or engine trouble must have stranded them and that we had better go ahead and get our job done.

Near a by-road east of Cahersiveen where the college stands we heard a police whistle and in the gleam of our headlights we saw two RIC men swinging a lantern. I remember grasping the .32 Savage I had borrowed from Joe Plunkett, my own Webley being a bit heavy for travelling, and I heard Dinny say, 'Will we shoot?'

'No,' says I, 'let someone else start the war. Talk will do these fellas.'

And sure enough so it did. Plausible speech and ready addresses in Limerick, cigarettes and a fill of tobacco got us through with the most perfunctory search of the car and an apology.

Medical students we were, *mar dheadh*, bound for Waterville, boots in the square box, clothes in the portmanteau.

'Good night gentlemen, sorry to trouble ye.' The car moved off and we breathed again. Half a mile along the road we stopped to see what really was in the box and bag. Oh sergeant, the box contained two jimmies, a keyhole saw and a few other such trinkets. The bag held electrical appliances, two hatchets and a heavy hammer.

Over the edge went the lot, owners having no further use for same. The job was off, a few words dropped by the sergeant had let out that a platoon of soldiers had come to guard the wireless college and that all police units were on patrol.

Nothing for it now but to get out of Kerry and no way out but Ballaghisheen 1200 feet up. So, for an hour, we climbed in the darkness up that narrow pass through the mountain bogland. At last we gained the crown of the pass, hours it had seemed to Dinny and myself shoving the old Maxwell up the hill.

'She'll do there til light comes' … Huddled together in the back of the car we slept until the chill of morning awoke us to a new struggle for life and liberty. So it happened that two dog-tired and disappointed lads lay full length on the seat of the 7.10 a.m. train leaving Killarney while two miles out the road Tom [*sic*] struggled with a burst tyre and a broken front spring, the fruits of injudicious mountaineering.[1]

It was in Belfast a full month afterwards that I read a newspaper yarn of a car in the river at Killorglin and three men drowned. Then, at last, I knew how my boys' odyssey had ended … They took the ford and I took the high road; they were drowned and I came safe.

---

1 Ó Lochlainn appears to have confused the names of the two drivers on the mission, Tom McInerney and Samuel Windrim. It was Samuel Windrim who drove Daly and Ó Lochlainn to Cahersiveen.

CASEMENT'S GERMAN VENTURE

Ryle Dwyer

Captain Karl Spindler, commander of the *Aud* and author of *The Mystery of the Casement Ship*. This portrait photograph was taken in Germany *c.* 1916. (Courtesy of Mercier Press)

ROGER Casement travelled to Germany in November 1914 to arrange German help to secure Irish independence. He asked the Germans to facilitate the formation of an Irish Brigade made up of the Irish soldiers and other Irishmen who were prisoners of war at that time in Germany. The Germans agreed, but Casement managed to recruit only fifty-six men from over 2,200 Irish prisoners of war. Two of those recruits were from Kerry – Lance Corporal David Golden and Private Frank Sewell, both of the Royal Munster Fusiliers.

Casement was also able to persuade the Germans to provide 20,000 rifles and ten machine guns for the proposed Easter Rising. The arms were to be shipped to Ireland by the German navy in a disguised Norwegian trader, the *Aud*, which left Lübeck on 9 April 1916, and were to be landed at Fenit between Holy Thursday and Easter Sunday (20–23 April 1916). The *Aud*'s skipper, Karl Spindler, had orders to pick up Casement from a submarine in Tralee Bay. 'I was then to proceed under his

Casement, seen here, bearded, standing in the centre of the group on top of the conning tower of U-19, while en route to Fenit.

instructions,' Spindler noted in *The Mystery of the Casement Ship*, a book he wrote about the episode.

The Germans wanted to send the fifty-six men recruited for the Irish Brigade to help with the Rising, but Casement would not hear of this. He was disillusioned with the Germans at that stage and was anxious to return to Ireland to stop the Rising, which he believed was doomed to failure. He would have preferred to return alone, but Robert Monteith, who had been sent to Germany to help organise the Irish Brigade, insisted on accompanying him. Monteith persuaded Casement to bring along Daniel Julian Bailey – a prisoner of war turned member of the Irish Brigade – because he could demonstrate how to use the machine guns in the arms shipment.

At Wilhelmshaven, on 12 April 1916, Casement, Monteith and Bailey boarded U-20, the German submarine which sank the *Lusitania* off the Cork coast eleven months earlier. However, they ran into mechanical difficulties and had to put into Helgoland, where the three Irishmen were transferred to U-19 and their journey continued. Two days after U-19 set out for Ireland, Berlin received a message from Dublin stipulating that the arms should not be landed at Fenit before Easter Sunday. Unfortunately the *Aud* had no radio, so Spindler was unaware that he was not expected until the end of the four-day window set for his arrival. He was planning to land the guns on the Thursday. The change of U-boats had cost valuable time, with the result that U-19 was still some hours behind when the *Aud* arrived in Tralee Bay on Holy Thursday afternoon.

U-19 arrived in the middle of the night and dispatched Casement and his two colleagues towards Banna Strand, a few miles north of Fenit, in a small, flat-bottomed boat made of wood with a canvas and rubber inflatable section. Nearing the shore, the boat capsized in the surf, throwing the men into the water, but they made it ashore between 3 a.m. and 4 a.m. on Good Friday. As Casement was suffering from a recurrence of malaria, he was in no condition to walk to Tralee, so Monteith and Bailey left him hiding in McKenna's Fort overlooking Curraghane and set off on foot towards the town.

Two RIC officers with the collapsible boat from U-19 that was used to land Casement, Monteith and Bailey on Banna Strand on Good Friday morning. (Courtesy of Mercier Press)

While waiting, Casement violated the first rule of hiding by failing to keep his head down. He was standing up in the fort looking towards the beach around 1.20 p.m. and did not see Constable Bernard O'Reilly of the RIC on the road behind him. 'When I first saw him his head and shoulders were appearing over some shrubbery in the fort,' O'Reilly later testified at Casement's trial.

The RIC in Ardfert had been informed that a boat had been found on the beach earlier that morning, with some weapons nearby, and that three men had been seen coming from the beach. O'Reilly and his sergeant, John Hearn, were searching the area around the fort where the three men had been seen. When challenged, Casement identified himself as Richard Morton from Denham,

Buckinghamshire, author of a book on the life of Saint Brendan. He said he had visited Mount Brandon, before arriving at the fort at 8 a.m. Sergeant Hearn decided to take him to the RIC station in Ardfert for questioning. Casement was so weak that they had to get young Martin Collins – who happened to come along the road in a pony and trap – to take them there. On the way they stopped to allow a local woman, Mary Gorman, to identify Casement as one of three men she saw coming from the beach early that morning, around 5.15 a.m.

Two RIC men then brought Casement to Tralee in a sidecar between 3 p.m. and 4 p.m. One of the constables was Jim Murphy, whose son Jas later captained Kerry to victory in the 1953 All-Ireland football final. John A. Kearney, the head constable in Tralee, recognised Casement from newspaper pictures he had seen and treated him kindly. He put him into a police recreation room with a fire, instead of a cold cell, and sent for a doctor to treat him.

'I went along and found a clean-shaven man of distinguished appearance sitting over a smoky fire in the policemen's billiards room,' Dr Mikey Shanahan recalled to *The Kerryman* in 1965. Once they were alone together, Casement identified himself 'and expressed the hope that I was in sympathy with the Irish cause'. Shanahan added:

> The impression I got was that I should tell the people outside that he was in the barracks and that he had no other purpose in mind only that he might be released which was quite an easy matter at that time. The barracks door was wide open and half a dozen men with revolvers could have walked in there and taken Sir Roger away.

As the doctor was about to leave the building, Kearney showed him a newspaper photograph of a bearded Casement and suggested it looked like the clean-shaven prisoner. 'Is not there a remarkable resemblance to the prisoner?' the head constable asked.

'I could see that Kearney knew that the man he had inside was Sir Roger, or was really suspicious that he was Sir Roger, but even so the prisoner was under no heavy guard,' the doctor noted. Kearney was giving Shanahan a subtle warning that the RIC suspected they had Casement, so the Volunteers had better act quickly.

Kearney invited Casement upstairs to his family quarters, and had his wife cook a steak dinner for him. Later in the evening Kearney sent a constable out to a nearby pub to get Casement a glass of whiskey as a nightcap.

The head constable 'was very friendly to me', Casement later told his lawyers. 'I said a lot of things to him during the night. Many of these things were in confidence, as at that time, I was bent on taking the poison I had, and wanted this friendly man to tell all my friends.' But because of Kearney's kindness, Casement decided not to go through with his suicide plans. When there was no sign of any rescue, he asked to speak to a priest. 'What do you want with a priest?' Kearney asked. 'Aren't you a Protestant?'

Nonetheless, Kearney summoned a priest from the nearby Dominican priory and allowed him to meet privately with the prisoner. Casement identified himself to Fr Francis Ryan and asked him to get a message to the Volunteers. 'Tell them I am a prisoner, and that the rebellion will be a dismal hopeless failure, as the help they expect will not arrive,' he said. Fr Ryan was taken aback. He had no desire to become involved in this kind of politics. 'Do what I ask,' Casement pleaded, 'and you will bring God's blessing on the country and on everyone concerned.'

Next morning Kearney had his wife cook breakfast for Casement, who was then taken through the streets of Tralee on foot, under a heavy RIC guard, to the railway station that now bears his name. He was put in a private carriage on the 10.30 a.m. train to Dublin in the custody of just one RIC man, Sergeant James Butler. Upon arrival in Dublin, Casement was promptly transferred by boat to Holyhead, from where he was taken to London by train.

On Easter Sunday he was questioned by Basil Thompson, head of the Criminal Investigative Division at Scotland Yard, and Admiral William 'Blinker' Hall, head of Naval Intelligence. Casement pleaded to be allowed to appeal to those in Dublin to call off the Rising, but they refused. According to Christopher Andrew's

Secret Service: The Making of the British Intelligence Community, Hall wished for the Rising to go ahead so that the London government would then suppress Irish nationalism. 'It is better that a cankering sore like this should be cut out,' he insisted.

Having agonised about Casement's request over the weekend, Fr Ryan passed on the message to Austin Stack's adjutant, Paddy Cahill, on Monday morning. By then the rebels were already forming in Dublin and it was much too late to have any impact. It seemed that Murphy's Law was in vogue in Kerry that weekend – anything that could go wrong, did go wrong.

THE FAILURE TO RESCUE CASEMENT

Ryle Dwyer

HAVING left Roger Casement at McKenna's Fort, Robert Monteith and Daniel Bailey reached Tralee on foot around 8 a.m. on Good Friday. Seeing a poster for *The Irish Volunteer* newspaper outside a shop in Dominick Street, they asked the owner, George Spicer, for help. Monteith said he wished to have the commander of the Tralee Volunteers informed that he had 'a very urgent message – a message which must be acted upon at once'. Austin Stack was notified at his residence in Lower Rock Street, but fearing it might be some kind of British trap, he took his time responding. It was after 9.30 a.m. before he arrived at Spicer's, along with Con Collins, a member of the Volunteers and the IRB, who was down from Dublin to make final arrangements for the distribution of the arms due at Fenit.

Collins recognised Monteith, thereby relieving their fears. Monteith told them that Casement had returned, wishing to 'transmit a message to headquarters' to call off the Rising because the Germans were not providing sufficient help. 'I explained that I could not accept these as Sir Roger Casement's views, without having them from his own lips,' Stack recalled in an article published in *The Kerry Champion* on 7 September 1929.

Around 11 a.m. Stack asked Maurice 'Mossy' Moriarty to drive Bailey, Collins and himself out to collect Casement. Moriarty later recounted in his BMH statement that Stack told him 'we don't know where he is but he is probably somewhere around Banna Strand'. As Stack and company entered the road leading to Banna, off the main Ardfert to Ballyheigue road, they noticed a policeman beside a horse dragging a cart in which was a boat. 'That is the boat we used after leaving the submarine,' Bailey said.

**Robert Monteith (*left*) and Daniel Bailey (*centre*) saluting Lieutenant Rudolf Zenter on the deck of U-20 shortly before the submarine departed from Germany.
(Courtesy of Mercier Press)**

'Oh, God, lads, the game is up,' Stack exclaimed.

'There were about twenty police there posted at different points,' according to Moriarty. RIC sergeant Daniel Crowley from Ballyheigue asked them what they were doing in the area. Moriarty said he was driving his passengers to Ballyheigue and showing them the area. Sergeant Crowley searched the car and allowed them to leave.

'We turned round the car, got back on the main road and proceeded towards Ballyheigue, away from the direction where Casement lay,' Stack recalled. 'The policeman had not his suspicions allayed and we found that he was following us on a bicycle. I got the driver to proceed at a good pace.' Although they had diverted the sergeant from the search for Casement, the latter was found by the RIC at around 1.20 p.m.

After Stack returned to Tralee, Dr Shanahan informed him in the early evening that Casement was in the RIC barracks and could easily be rescued, but Stack felt unable to attempt a rescue because Patrick Pearse had insisted that there should be no trouble in the Tralee area before the arms were landed at Fenit on Sunday. 'Austin was blamed by some for not trying to organise a rescue of Sir Roger Casement and I know he felt very sore about it,' his wife, Una, later explained in her BMH statement. 'He always said his orders were definite that no shot should be fired before the start of general hostilities on Easter Sunday and he knew well that any fracas that might take place in Tralee would frustrate all the plans made for the Rising.'

Michael O'Flynn, the Gaelic League organiser for Kerry, also informed Stack that the head constable had taken Con Collins to the RIC barracks for questioning. As RIC County Inspector Hugh Hill noted in his later report of the incident, written on 11 May, '[Collins's] answers being very unsatisfactory, I directed the Head Constable to arrest him'. He then instructed Kearney to arrest Stack. 'But before this was done Stack came to the barracks to see Collins,' according to Hill.

'O'Flynn told me that Mr Collins wished to speak to me at the Police barrack, and that the Head Constable had said this would be all right – that Collins would be allowed to see me,' Stack noted. Paddy Cahill, Stack's adjutant, urged him not to go.'I told him he would not be allowed out if he went there,'Cahill later recalled. 'I took his revolver (auto) and about a hundred rounds of ammunition from him and he looked through his papers and said he had nothing of importance on him.' Yet Stack later wrote to his brother, Nicholas, that he was carrying two pocket books,'besides a large number of letters, i.e. fully 20 or 30 letters I imagine'. These included letters from Eoin MacNeill, James Connolly, Bulmer Hobson and Patrick Pearse.

County Inspector Hill had already ordered Stack's arrest, so those documents were not actually a factor in his detention. But why was he carrying them? Possibly to ensure his arrest before the Rising as things were already going wrong.

Head Constable Kearney visited Stack in his cell during the night: 'That is a very interesting man we have upstairs,' Kearney said.

'I suspected from the commencement that the Head Constable was looking for some clue as to the identity of the prisoner, and I decided not to give him any assistance,' Stack noted. Of course, Kearney already knew the prisoner was Casement:

> The Head Constable came to me a second time during the night, and tried to speak to me very confidentially, and told me that he believed the person whom they had to be no less a person than Sir Roger Casement, and that Casement has been asking about me. I did not give him any encouragement, on this occasion either, simply saying, that even if Casement had been speaking with him, he could not have mentioned my name, as he had not even heard of me.

Kearney later demonstrated his Irish nationalism when he facilitated the intelligence operations of Michael Collins during the War of Independence, so did Stack spurn a last chance to help Casement?

CASEMENT'S LEGACY

Brian Ó Conchubhair

ROGER Casement spent less than thirty-six hours in North Kerry and the majority of that period was as a prisoner in Tralee. Having disembarked from U-19 in the early hours of Friday 21 April 1916, he departed Tralee railway station on Saturday morning, 22 April, accompanied by a minor official of the British Empire. Whichever thread of his remarkable life one follows – knight of the realm, world-renowned human rights activist, criminal investigator, anti-imperial critic, co-founder of the Irish Volunteers – they inescapably conclude in Kerry.

Despite the brevity of his stint in Kerry, he looms large in the county's collective memory. In Casement, all of Kerry, regardless of political affiliation, had a hero who would be embraced and lauded. As Lucy McDiarmid has written in her essay 'Secular Relics: Casement's Boat, Casement's Dish', Casement's landing at Banna transformed the strand and surrounding area into 'a charismatic landscape, a place of supernatural power, a point of pilgrimage'. The place-names of North Kerry reflect Casement's prominent status in the region's cultural memory: Casement's Fort, Casement View, Casement's Villas, Casement's Avenue, Sir Roger's Caravan Park, Casement railway station, Gaelscoil Mhic Easmainn. Artefacts, including the boat in which he allegedly came ashore, the *Aud*'s anchor, the platter from which he ate his last meal before his execution in Pentonville Prison in London, and his sword and ceremonial uniform, are all frequently displayed within the county. An imposing oil portrait hangs in Casement station in Tralee. Banna Strand is home to a privately built monument, which has been maintained by the National Graves Association since 2012. Ballyheigue vaunts a sculpture by no less a distinguished artist than Oisín Kelly, whose sculptures also appear on O'Connell Street and in the Garden of Remembrance in Dublin. Yet Ardfert, the village closest to the epicentre of Casement's dramatic capture at Banna, has neither memorial nor statue, thus neatly illustrating McDiarmid's contention that the 'national Irish collective memory of Casement is itself complex and disturbed'.

Ireland chose to celebrate a version of Casement which was nationalist, humanitarian, heterosexual and Catholic. But Casement's legacy is as contested as it is considerable, as pliable as it is potent. Controversy stalks the entire course of his life. Doubts and discrepancies pervade his baptism, religious views, dramatic conversion to Catholicism, sexual orientation and failed efforts to prevent the Rising while importing weapons to Ireland. Such complexities allow interest groups and pressure groups to choose selectively and promote a particular version of Casement, the version that advances their particular agenda – gay rights groups, Catholic groups, human rights groups, language activists, eco-warriors, republicans, socialists, liberals and cultural nationalists.

Casement remains in the eye of the public storm because the complexities and controversies that engulfed him remain alive today and he is as much a lightning rod in death as he was in life. Throughout his life Casement was a contentious figure: championing unpopular causes, challenging vested interests and campaigning against the status quo. Long after the other fifteen executed leaders of the Rising were dead and buried, the issue of Casement's remains dogged Anglo-Irish relations. Even when his body was repatriated, controversy surrounded the exhumation process and the preferred location of the reinternment.

Just as doubts surrounded his preferred landing place (Fenit or An Cheathrú Rua, Galway), a Royal Irish Academy investigation failed to resolve conclusively the questions over the authenticity of the diaries associated with Casement – were the 'Black Diaries' forged, amended or doctored? Was Casement straight or gay? Does it matter? If so, to whom and why?

With the possible exception of James Connolly, the story of the other executed leaders is an Irish affair – where Irish-born nationalists following IRB traditions sought to break the link with Great Britain through violence rather than through the constitutional politics advocated by the IPP. While other 1916 leaders can be largely rationalised as Irish republicans, Casement is complicated, and much more so for our neighbours across the Irish Sea. He was, after all, an imperial agent and a knight of the realm, not a disaffected Irish nationalist experiencing blocked social and professional mobility. So he cannot be understood in terms of one single overriding ideology.

A member of the British elite, Casement turned his back on all the benefits that entailed in order to pursue his dream of a free Ireland. He risked more than any other 1916 leader in his engagement with Irish nationalism. His nationalist commitments in Ireland were a product of, rather than a diversion from, his internationalist concerns for human rights in the imperial world. A career diplomat in the British Colonial Service, his duties brought him to Africa and South America and what he witnessed there – abuse, torture, exploitation – transformed him into Europe's, if not the world's, most prominent human rights activist of the late nineteenth and early twentieth centuries.

In the Congo, he administered a region approximately two-thirds the size of Europe. But his experiences

A handcuffed Roger Casement is seen here being escorted to court during his trial on charges of high treason in London. (Courtesy of Mercier Press)

there, and in Peru, radicalised him. A new political consciousness saw the formerly pro-British imperialist resign from the Colonial Service in 1913, align himself with the burgeoning Irish revolutionary movement and become a founding member of the Irish Volunteers. Casement was, and remains, a humanitarian and a political figure of extraordinary importance.

In August 1917 crowds gathered at McKenna's Fort to hear Thomas Ashe honour the first anniversary of Casement's execution for high treason. In April 2016 throngs again convened at Banna to celebrate Casement's patriotism and humanitarianism. When people gathered to remember and honour Casement staggering through the white waves at Banna in the morning darkness, stumbling through the dunes and lying ill among the primroses and violets of McKenna's Fort, did anyone spare a thought for those others who were then staggering through waves and stumbling onto Greek shores, fleeing war and persecution in Syria, Afghanistan and Iraq? When lauding Casement for his exposure of the inhumane and racist treatment of native peoples in Africa and South America, will anyone consider what Casement – who risked the ire of kings and rubber barons in exposing injustice and inhumanity – would say of the contemporary treatment of religious and ethnic minorities in Ireland?

How would Casement respond to the finding of the European Network Against Racism (Ireland) that social media is increasingly being used to abuse minorities and to mobilise racism? How would Casement react to the verbal abuse of an African woman displaying a Kerry flag on her car, as occurred in late 2015? Where would Casement stand on the discrimination against and negative treatment of Irish Travellers and Roma? What would he say about the current levels of human trafficking in Ireland? We extoll Casement's generosity to malnourished Irish children in Antrim and Galway, but what would he say about state-born policies that discriminate against Irish children by refusing them access to state-funded schools? Where would Casement stand on these controversial issues?

In his famous poem 'The Ghost of Roger Casement', W. B. Yeats wrote that

'The ghost of Roger Casement is beating on the door.' Do we now hear that ghost or do we choose to ignore Casement's legacy even as we seek to celebrate him? In commemorating him are we compartmentalising what he embodied?

It was Casement's fellow patriot P. H. Pearse who wrote in his pamphlet *Christmas Ghosts*, in December 1915, of the legacy of Irish republicanism:

> There is only one way to appease a ghost. You must do the thing it asks you. The ghosts of a nation sometimes ask very big things; and they must be appeased, whatever the cost.

Do the ideals and principles of Casement, Pearse, Connolly and those who signed Forógra na Poblachta/the 1916 Proclamation have any relevance today? These ideas and principles are outlined in the Proclamation:

> We declare the right of the people of Ireland to the ownership of Ireland and to the unfettered control of Irish destinies … The Republic guarantees religious and civil liberty, equal rights and equal opportunities to all its citizens … cherishing all of the children of the nation equally …

So what and whom exactly are we celebrating when we commemorate Casement and the 1916 Rising: actions or ideals? Motives or results?

STACK VERDICT WAS A TRAVESTY

Ryle Dwyer

WHEN Austin Stack was arrested at the RIC barracks in Tralee on Good Friday 1916, he was carrying a large bundle of letters on his person. These were

Irish Volunteers, including Austin Stack, at Tralee Sportsfield (now Austin Stack Park).
Front row: (left to right): Danny Healy, Austin Stack, Alfred Cotton.
Middle row: Michael Doyle, Frank Roche, Danny Mullins, Eddie Barry.
Back row: Joe Meelin, Ned Lynch, Mick Fleming. (Courtesy of Mercier Press)

later introduced in evidence against him at his court martial, which began at Richmond Barracks, Dublin, on Thursday 15 June 1916.

The prosecution highlighted a letter from James Connolly to Stack written on 6 December 1915. 'It is not our purpose to disrupt, but rather to enforce and strengthen the true National movement,' Connolly wrote, 'and in a town the size of Tralee, there is no necessity for any other military body than the Volunteer Corps which has stood out so splendidly by the true Irish ideal – the corps that you command.'

In outlining his case for the court, the prosecutor, Major Edmund G. Kimber, mentioned a sensational printed article that was enclosed with Connolly's letter. This material ridiculed the idea that war could be humanised: 'You might as well talk of humanising hell!' the writer claimed. It was absurd to think that war could be civilised, the article argued. 'The essence of war is violence; moderation in war is imbecility; hit first, hit hard, and hit everywhere … Hit your enemy in the belly and kick him when he is down, and boil your prisoners in oil and torture his women and children; then people will keep clear of you.'

It was bloodthirsty stuff that provided a gripping introduction to the case against Stack and Con Collins, who had been arrested in Tralee on the evening of 21 April 1916. The men were charged with conspiring with others to bring about a rebellion in Ireland and spread disaffection among the civil population with the intent of helping the enemy. They were also charged with harbouring Robert Monteith and Daniel Bailey, who had arrived on the submarine with Roger Casement, and trying to assist them in importing arms illegally for use in the Rising.

The prosecution contended that, in relation to both charges, Stack and Collins were trying to help the enemy, Germany. Both were aware that the Germans were supposed to land arms at Fenit on Easter Sunday. In fact, Collins had come from Dublin to help organise the distribution of those arms.

The first two days of the case were taken up largely with procedural arguments, as King's Counsel Edward J. McElligott, a native of Listowel who was representing Stack and Collins, challenged the jurisdiction of the military court. Stack and Collins had been taken into the custody of the civil power on Good Friday, over two days before the Rising began. Consequently, McElligott argued, the military court had no jurisdiction in their case. He even cited the case of Wolfe Tone in 1798 as a precedent. Tone had been arrested by the military, but he was handed over and tried by the civil authority. McElligott insisted that Stack and Collins should therefore be tried before a jury in a civil court.

Major-General Lord Cheylesmore, who presided at the court martial, suspended the hearing overnight. The following day he ruled that the case should go ahead.

During the court martial Head Constable John A. Kearney testified about arresting both Collins and Stack. In cross-examining Kearney about Stack's correspondence, McElligott referred to printed material enclosed in the Connolly letter that was quoted by the prosecutor. 'You will agree that the newspaper cutting which Major Kimber read in his opening statement is a very brutal document?'

'I should say so,' Kearney replied.

'Did the prisoner tell you that it was an extract from *The Review of Reviews* of February 1910?' McElligott asked.

'No,' said Kearney.

'Or that the article in the *Review* professed to give the very words as the sentiments of Admiral Lord Fisher?'

'Yes; he said they were the words of Lord Fisher.'

A copy of the magazine was handed to Kearney, who, at McElligott's request, read out the extract that Kimber had quoted in his opening statement.

Despite the fact that the bloodthirsty article had not been written by Connolly, but by the First Sea Lord of the Admiralty, Admiral John Fisher, Stack and Collins were sentenced to life in prison by the military court the following week. 'What for?' one might ask. They had played no part whatsoever in the *Aud* fiasco, and had abandoned efforts to rescue Casement while he was still in hiding. Stack even blocked any effort to rescue him in Tralee. The sentence was a farce, but then what happened to Casement, who had come with the intention of stopping the Rising, was an even greater perversion of true justice.

COURT MARTIAL ON MESSRS AUSTIN STACK AND CON COLLINS

Saturday 24 June 1916

Dublin, Friday.

Austin Stack, solicitor's clerk, Tralee, and Cornelius Collins, described as a clerk in the G.P.O., Dublin, were again before a general court martial, presided over by Major-General Lord Cheylesmore, at Richmond Barracks, to-day, the charge against the accused being that in or about the month of April, 1916, they conspired with certain other disloyal and disaffected persons to bring about rebellion in Ireland and to spread disaffection among the civilian population with the intention and for the purpose of assisting the enemy.

Secondly, that in or about the month of April, knowing or having reasonable grounds for supposing that certain persons, by name Monteith and Bailey, were then engaged in the importation of arms and ammunition without the previous permit of the competent naval or military authority, they harboured Monteith and Bailey, such act being committed with the intention and for the purpose of assisting the enemy.

The case was adjourned until to-day, in consequence of an objection to the jurisdiction of the court, raised by counsel for the accused on the grounds that they were in the custody of the civil power prior to any disturbance in Ireland and there was no jurisdiction to take them out of the civil custody and try them by courtmartial.

Mr K. Marshal was Judge Advocate. Major Kimber DSO (instructed by Mr Robinson of the Chief Crown Solicitor's office) prosecuted. Mr McElligott K.C. and Mr Arthur Clery (instructed by Mr John O'Connell, LLD, Tralee) appeared for the defence.

ECHO OF WOLFE TONE COUNSEL'S GROUND OF OBJECTION OVER-RULED.

At the sitting of the Court this morning, Mr McElligott, K.C., called

Mr McCarthy, C.P.S., Tralee. Major Kimber objected to the procedure as the grounds of the objection had not been stated.

Mr McElligott said that he grounded his objection to the trial by that tribunal on the fact that the accused were in the custody of the civil power on April 26 when they were taken out of that custody by the military. They were legally in the custody of the civil power from April 21 and on that date had been remanded on a specified charge and handed over to the governor of the civil prison where they were detained until the military authorities took charge of them for the purpose of having them tried by court martial.

The President – Will you state the legal grounds of your objection?

Mr McElligott said that under the Defence of the Realm Act there was no provision for the handing over of prisoners by the civil power to the military power. He submitted that both the civil and military power acted illegally and that the only tribunal before which the accused could be tried was a judge and jury. He cited a number of cases in support of his argument, among them being the CASE OF WOLFE TONE, decided in 1798. Wolfe Tone was in the custody of the military authorities and a writ of habeas corpus was moved for on the King's Bench. The writ was held to lie, and Wolfe Tone was taken from military custody and tried by the civil power.

Mr McCarthy, Clerk of the Petty Sessions at Tralee, Mr McHugh, Governor of Tralee Prison, and District Inspector Britten, Tralee, having given formal evidence, Major Kimber replied to Mr McElligott's arguments.

The President said the point was a most important one and the Court retired to consult. On returning to Court, the President said they had considered the objection and decided to overrule it, and proceed with the trial.

The accused were then formally charged, and pleaded not guilty.

HUE AND CRY. TALE OF THE ARREST OF MESSRS STACK AND COLLINS.

Major Kimber, on opening the case for the prosecution, said the accused man, Stack, was a well-known commander of the Irish Volunteers and Collins was a clerk in the employment of his Majesty in the Dublin Post Office. The events referred to in the charge against the men occurred immediately before the rebellion. These men were in touch with people who came to this country in company with German bluejackets who were taken prisoner in Cork and interned.

Proceeding the prosecutor said that at 2 o'clock on the afternoon of the 20th April, an old pilot was in his garden and saw a two-masted steamer coming into Scraggane, a point on the Western side of Tralee Bay. She came in from the N.N.W. dead slow, and presently moved out again, shaping her course for Loophead. She crossed to the west, and presently to the south again, and at sundown the old pilot saw her about two miles out with head east and stopped. He watched her until 11 p.m. She put up no lights but lay there. At 6 o'clock in the morning he saw her again, and watched her until half-past 11 when she went out of sight.

In tracing the movements of the vessel afterwards, the prosecutor said that later in the day she was outside Cork. A boat put off from her with three German officers and some German bluejackets who were taken prisoners by a pilot boat. The boat herself was sunk by her own crew, and she contained arms and ammunition from Germany to aid the rebellion in this country. In the early morning, while his vessel was opposite the pilot's house, a small farmer left his house at Currahane, west of Ardfert and, it being Good Friday, he sets out for a holy well. On his return, about 4 o'clock in the morning, he found on the shore a flat-bottomed boat with four oars.

In the boat was a dagger and close by in the sands a tin can and the footmarks of three men. Later were discovered three Mauser pistols, a flag, map and hand-bags. The farmer got assistance and pulled the boat up to the shore. At 4.30 o'clock [sic], a girl named Mary Gorman saw three men go slowly past the house where she worked, proceeding in the direction of Ardfert. One was a tall, dark man, subsequently identified as Sir Roger Casement. The story was next picked up in Tralee, where early that morning, two strangers entered a newspaper shop and asked for the local commander of the Irish Volunteers. One of them gave the name of Murray, but it was afterwards found out that his real name was Capt. Monteith. The other, who gave the name of Mulcahy, turned out to be Bailey. Messages were apparently sent out to Irish Volunteers and the two accused men, Stack and Collins arrived, no doubt, in reply to these messages. Stack, Collins and Monteith had a conference in the parlour of the house and Bailey remained in the kitchen. The first man to leave was Stack, who went to make arrangements for a motor car and later Bailey and Collins left, and Monteith remained in the house, where he stopped for a considerable time and had refreshments. Meanwhile, the Irish Volunteers assembled and he was taken to the hall of the Hibernian Organisation. At eleven o'clock that morning, Stack, Collins and Bailey set out in a motor car in the direction of Ballyheigue.

The prosecutor, continuing, said he would follow the fortunes of another of the men. When the boat was found on the shore and the pistols and other things, a hue and cry was raised and a sergeant and constable found Sir Roger Casement in an old fort between Ardfert and Currahane. There were sandwiches there made of German sausages and black bread (laughter). At eleven o'clock Stack, Collins and Bailey set out in the car for the search of Sir Roger Casement.

The chauffeur would be examined and tell them that when they got close to where the boat was found, he was ordered to turn to the left. Afterwards, the tyre burst and the noise attracted the police and the occupants of the car were questioned. They said they were going to Ballyheigue further north. They endeavoured to evade the police, but were unable to do so. It transpired that they were unable to find Casement.

At one point Bailey left them. The car was driven to a point turning in the direction of Tralee and stopped and a search was made by the police. The prisoner, Collins, stated that he was in the accountant's office at the GPO and that he spent some of his holidays in Tralee and that he was a friend of Mulcahy's with whom he had been. That referred to

Bailey. Further he said that they met a cyclist and it would be shown that when arrested, that prisoner was found in possession of a revolver and 33 rounds of ammunition and a sum of £35 in notes and cash. He stated that he carried the revolver in Dublin as he had to do business at night. Stack was arrested after a message had been sent to him from Collins. A soldier's English-German dictionary had been found on one of the prisoners. Amongst the documents found was one which would be proved was directed to Stack, which was signed by James Connolly who was one of the signatories to the Irish Rebellion Proclamation.

There was also found a cutting from a newspaper which contained the words:

'Humanising war – you might as well talk of humanising hell.' And again: 'My reply was considered unfit for publication, as if war could be civilised.'

'The essence of war is violence – moderation in war is an impossibility.'

'Hit your enemy in the belly and kick him while he is down and boil your prisoners in oil.'

Another document was a plan showing the position of the telephones and telegraph wires – in order, no doubt, that they might be more readily cut. He would submit to the court that the plan found was one whereby the landing was to be effected with arms and ammunition by the German bluejackets and Casement. Further, it would appear there was an arrangement of a code and information conveyed as to food supplies and other matters. If the court examined the map they would see it indicated a line across country to facilitate those engaged in reaching where the landing was to be effected. One document contained the words:

At the end of the peninsula have canoe ready,

and, further the words:

Destroy railway and bridges.

Those documents would be made evidence.

Head Constable Kearney, Tralee, said that he knew Austin Stack for the past three years and saw him marching with the Irish Volunteers and acting as commander. The Irish Volunteers of Tralee numbered about

200. He remembered a meeting held at Tralee of the Volunteers and addressed by a man named Partridge. On the 21st April he questioned Collins who told him he was a clerk in the GPO and that he had come there for a holiday, and had gone for a motor-drive with Stack and Mulcahy.

'FORM OF OATH'.

Witness arrested and charged him, and searched him. Collins gave him a revolver. On him, he found £35 and a dictionary – a soldier's English-German dictionary. Collins said he wanted to see Stack, who was then arrested and searched. He found documents and papers on him, including a map of Tralee with roads and telegraph lines marked. He also found a form of oath.

> I swear in presence of God, that I will become a member of the Irish Volunteers and do all in my power to assert the independence of Ireland.

This was written in shorthand:

> 'I will keep all secrets whatever they are and obey the commands of my superior officers.'

There were also notes of a meeting in pencil. He also found a letter on him addressed, 'Dear Mr Stack,' from the American Committee, Irish Volunteers, New York. It contained the sentence, 'The news from Ireland that recruiting is a failure, is very gratifying' and was signed by Patrick J. Griffin. In a letter from British East Africa were the words, 'Now is the moment for Young Ireland to assert itself.' One letter was signed 'Bulmer Hobson' and another by P. H. Pearse, and a further one by James Connolly.

In cross-examination, witness said the Volunteers had been drilling openly for months without interference. There was a fear of conscription being applied to the country, and the Volunteers took a strong line against it. One document was an extract from a newspaper.

SENTIMENTS OF ADMIRAL FISHER.

Mr McElligott said it was an extract from the 'Review of Reviews' of Feb. 1910 and professed to give the sentiments of Admiral Lord Fisher. It contained the following:–

> 'If you rub it in both at home and abroad that you are ready for instant war with every unit of your strength in a first line, and intend to be first in and hit your enemy in the belly, kick him when he is down and boil your prisoner in oil (if you take any), and torture his women and children, then people will keep clear of you.'

Constable P. O'Connell said that when Stack was taken into custody and told that Collins had been shadowed by witness, he replied, 'We will remember that for you.'

Mr S. H. Harrison said the salary of Collins was 47s 6d. He was entitled to 21 days' holidays, and selected from April 14 to May 11.

To Mr Clery – His record was satisfactory.

Det. Officer Crotty, G. Div., proved the association of Collins with the Sinn Féin leader.

The court then adjourned to this (Saturday) morning.

Dublin, Saturday Evening.

The courtmartial on Messrs. Austin Stack, Tralee and Cornelius Collins, was resumed at Richmond Barracks today.

Mr George Spicer, newsagent, Tralee, re-called and said Captain Monteith stayed behind in his house for some time after the others leaving. Monteith read the 'Kerry News', in which it was stated that a capture of arms had been made at Ardfert.

Major Kimber – Did Monteith say anything about it?

Mr McElligott, K.C., objected and the question was disallowed by the court.

The President then read a statement by Mr Austin Stack, in which he said he had always been a believer in the right of Ireland to self-government, and was prepared to support it by means similar to those adopted in Ulster against Home Rule. He had been an ardent worker in the Irish Volunteer movement. As to Monteith and Bailey, these men might have come from Timbuctoo [*sic*] as far as he was concerned or knew. He protested most strongly that he ever made use of the expression attributed to him by the constable.

The book given in evidence was a soldier's German-English dictionary which had been purchased for one penny at Ponsonby's, Dublin.

Mr C. Collins also handed in a written statement in which he stated that he was in Tralee on holidays and had no knowledge of a contemplated landing of arms. He had not been a member of any body of Volunteers for eighteen months.

Messrs. M. J. Flavin and T. O'Donnell, M.P.s gave evidence as to Mr Stack's high character, as did Mr T. J. Liston, solr. and Very Rev. Father O'Quigley, O.P., formerly Prior at Tralee.

Mr McElligott, K.C., then addressed the court and said that neither prisoner had ever seen Monteith or Bailey until the morning of the 21st April. There was no evidence that these men were concerned in the landing of arms.

The result of the Courtmartial would have an effect far and wide throughout the country whether for good or evil.

The court returned to consider their verdict and after an absence of a quarter of an hour, the President announced that the proceedings in public court had concluded and the prisoners were then removed.

VALENTIA AND THE RING BROTHERS

Courtesy of Valentia Island Tourist Office

THE impressive cable station building situated at Knightstown in Valentia Island is testament to the transatlantic cable laid between the American continent and Ireland in the mid-1860s, with every message from the summer of 1866 up to the 1920s crossing the Atlantic passing through the station at Valentia. However, many are unaware of the significant role played by the station in the 1916 Rising, a role that led to the rebels' allies in America and Germany learning that the Rising had begun before the British fully realised that Dublin was in arms.

This is the intriguing story of two Valentia Island brothers who acted as liaison officers between Patrick Pearse and John Devoy, leader of the republican Clan na Gael organisation in the United States. The remarkable fact is that the two brothers were operating from the most closely guarded communications centre of the British Empire during the First World War, as the station was the central communications terminus for the British before and at the outbreak of the war. A huge garrison of troops was dispatched to the island and barbed wire, military tents, guns, searchlight posts and all that went with war was quickly erected. The war at sea ensured that there could be no reliable contact by surface mail, so the cable station was the only sure method of keeping in touch with Washington and New York by way of the opposite cable terminus at Heart's Content in Canada. The British need for transatlantic communication to America was huge as they desperately tried to involve the United States in the war in Europe, where they were sorely pressed.

The need of the Dublin-based IRB to keep in touch with its opposite number in the United States, Clan na Gael, was equally as important. Pearse and his republican colleagues realised the need for skilled and patriotic men to liaise with Clan na Gael in America from the strategic outpost.

Tim and Eugene Ring of Valentia had been telegraphers from their youth, with the 'cable' being in the family tradition. Their grandfather operated as a telegrapher in the formative years of the station, with their father, Jeremiah, being one of the cable company's executives in Valentia. Tim Ring had been a member of the IRB for several years and he enlisted his brother's help – also an IRB member – in sending the message announcing the start of the Rising. With the assistance of their first cousin, Rosalie Rice, who worked at Kenmare Post Office, the Rings were able to send a telegram from Kenmare Post Office via the Valentia cable station to New York alerting the Americans to this momentous event.

On the morning of Easter Monday a Miss McGowan, who worked as a housekeeper-secretary for John Devoy in America, received the coded message from Valentia: 'Mother operated on successfully today'. The message was signed 'Kathleen'.

The Ring brothers had got their message across but, unfortunately, British Intelligence learned about this from a report in the *Gaelic American* newspaper, which said that news of the Rising had been sent to America 'from a remote corner of the Kerry coast'. They honed in on the cable station, resulting in the arrest of the brothers, who were among the few native Irish on the staff. Tim was jailed with his 1916 colleagues in Frongoch Internment Camp; Eugene, referred to locally as 'Euge', was incarcerated in Cahersiveen Barracks.

After their release, Eugene went on the run, fighting the Black and Tans in the War of Independence and taking the republican side in the Civil War. He later became a news correspondent for Irish and American papers. Eugene was also deeply involved in the GAA, holding a number of administrative roles, including the position of first secretary of the Valentia Young Islanders GAA club at the time of its foundation in 1905. Years later, Tim, who also played a limited role in the War of Independence, was reinstated to his job in the cable station.

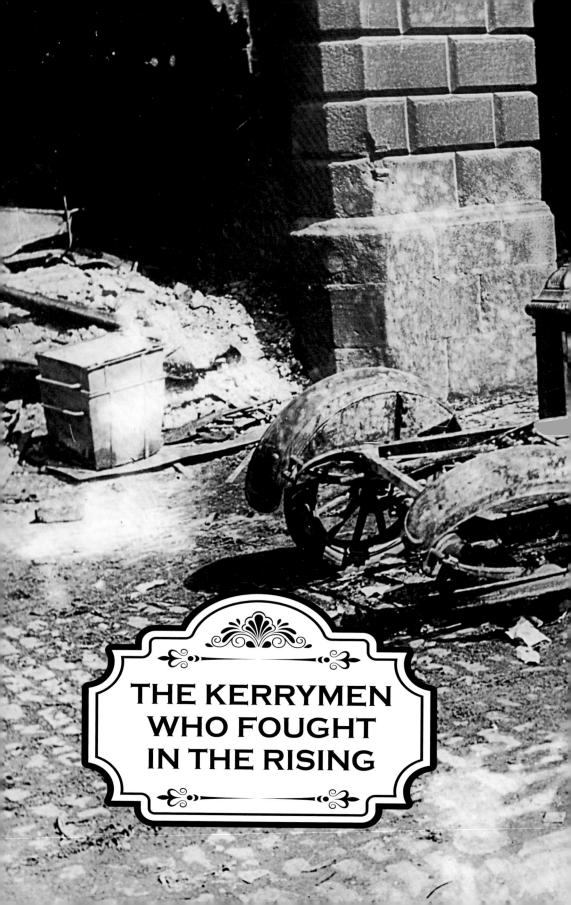

THE KERRYMEN
WHO FOUGHT
IN THE RISING

COMMANDANT THOMAS ASHE

Hélène O'Keeffe

ON Friday 28 April 1916 forty men of the 5th (Fingal) Battalion, Dublin Brigade, under Commandant Thomas Ashe, engaged a convoy of RIC officers at Rath Cross, a mile outside the village of Ashbourne in County Meath. After five hours of intense, close-quarter fighting, the RIC men surrendered to the North County Dublin Volunteers. In the words of Ashe's niece, Eileen Quinn, 'It was the one place they could say we had a battle and won. They just walked away.'

Born near Lispole in County Kerry on 12 January 1885, Thomas was the seventh of Gregory and Ellen Ashe's ten children. He grew up on his father's smallholding overlooking Dingle Bay where Gregory Ashe modelled the ideals of self-reliance and hard work, and nurtured in his children a strong sense of their Gaelic heritage.

Eileen's father, also Gregory, was 'five or six years younger' than Thomas, but shared the same defining elements of a rural Kerry upbringing at the close of the nineteenth century. Gregory told his daughter, for example, about the seasonal visit to the Ashe farm of a 'smallish, stout' travelling lady 'who came to spin the wool' after the sheep had been shorn. She stayed in the house and 'worked all the daylight hours'.

> My father said she held the wool between her big toe and the next toe and guided it through her foot, up to the [spinning] wheel. She turned the handle with her hand and thus, at the other end, came out the wool … She smoked a little dudeen [a clay pipe] … [and] could spit from the dross of the pipe into the fire without ever taking the pipe out of her mouth. As children, this was the funniest thing they had ever seen.

Eileen also recalled the influence of Kerry's travelling musicians and credits her uncle's love of music to the fact that 'from a young age, the [Ashe children] listened to other people singing and dancing and playing a melodeon or a whistle'. An accomplished storyteller and poet, Gregory instilled early in his children a love of language. Thomas and his sister Nora proved particularly adept students and both pursued careers in teaching – a family vocation which Eileen, also a teacher, traces to a paternal ancestor who was a 'hedge school teacher'.

In March 1908 Thomas secured a job as headmaster of the national school in Corduff, North County Dublin. A popular teacher, re-membered by many of his former pupils as fair and even-handed, Ashe was, according to Lieutenant Joseph Lawless of the Swords Company in his BMH statement, invested from the beginning 'in all the various phases of the national movement in Fingal'. He be-came a member of the hurling team in Lusk, founded the Black Raven Pipers' Band and set up branches of the Gaelic League in the North County Dublin villages. He also introduced his fervent nationalism to the classroom, as il-lustrated by his sister Nora's testimony to the BMH that when the children went outside for recreation, 'he used to get them to march over a Union Jack'. Eileen added that her uncle in-vited many notable speakers, including Roger Casement, to address the students at Corduff.

Thomas Ashe, standing pipe in hand, c. 1917. (Courtesy of Mercier Press)

A member of the IRB and an early recruit to the Irish Volunteers, Ashe was appointed adjutant of the 5th (Fingal) Battalion, Dublin Brigade, under Commandant Richard Hayes. Ashe also sat on the Gaelic League's governing body (An Coiste Gnótha) and in the spring of 1914 he was chosen to undertake a fund-raising mission on behalf of the Gaelic League to the United States, where he was briefly reunited with his brother Gregory, who had emigrated in 1912. They had a few days together in Boston, which, Eileen said, 'they enjoyed immensely', but Thomas returned to Ireland at the outbreak of the First World War and he did not see his brother again.

In September 1914 the combined strength of the Lusk, Swords, St Margaret's and Skerries companies of the 5th Battalion was just over 100 men. They carried out training and field exercises in conjunction with the city battalions and, in the months before the Rising, they acquired, according to Volunteer Michael McAllister of the Swords Company, 'a few good Lee Enfield Service Rifles' and an assortment of revolvers and automatic pistols to bolster the cache of Mauser rifles they had received after a large quantity of these guns were landed at Howth in July 1914.

In early April 1916 Hayes stepped down as commandant in favour of his thirty-one-year-old adjutant, Ashe, who, as the local IRB centre, had a close association with the Supreme Council of that organisation, making him the more influential figure. Hayes assumed the dual roles of battalion adjutant and medical officer to the column.

Despite the publication of Eoin MacNeill's countermanding order calling off the Rising on Easter Sunday, 120 men of the 5th Battalion turned out to parade at Saucerstown in Swords. When official orders failed to arrive, a frustrated Ashe entrusted eighteen-year-old Joseph Lawless with a dispatch for James Connolly in Liberty Hall. Lawless later recalled, 'As some speed was necessary in the matter, Ashe told me to take his motor cycle, an almost new two-stroke "New Hudson", which I had ridden before and was therefore familiar with. So, very conscious of the importance of my mission, I rode off, reaching Dublin within twenty minutes or so.' Lawless returned on Sunday evening with Connolly's orders to 'stand to' and Ashe demobilised his battalion with instructions to await further orders.

At 7 a.m. on Monday, Cumann na mBan member Mary Lawless delivered Pearse's order to 'Strike at one o'clock today'. Ashe immediately issued orders for the mobilisation of the four North County Dublin companies, but the confusion caused by conflicting orders meant that only fifty men paraded at Knocksedan Cross. Volunteers returning from the Fairyhouse Races joined them during the afternoon, and by evening there were between sixty and seventy men under Ashe's command working to fortify their encampment situated in farmland two miles south of Finglas.

Ashe's strategy, similar to that adopted in Dublin, was to occupy and defend a fixed position and send out cycle units to disable communications and destroy important railway targets. Richard Mulcahy, a lieutenant in the 3rd Battalion, joined them on Monday evening, along with two other Volunteers, Tom Maxwell and Paddy Grant. These three men had been assigned the task of destroying the communication lines at Howth Junction, but, on the way back, found that they were unable to link up with their own unit in the city. Forced to make a detour to avoid two policemen, they ended up in Finglas golf course, where they were picked up by Ashe's men. The Volunteers settled in for the night, encouraged by the news – carried by Mollie Adrian – that the Republic had been declared in Dublin.

At 10 a.m. the next morning Ashe received orders from James Connolly to organise diversionary raids and to send forty men to reinforce the city garrisons. Reluctant to reduce the battalion strength so significantly, Ashe dispatched half that number into Dublin under the command of Captain Richard Coleman. With Mulcahy, his newly appointed second-in-command, Ashe proceeded to organise the remaining battalion into four mobile columns or 'sections' of approximately twelve men each.

In the days that followed, the two men led the Fingal Volunteers in what historian Fearghal McGarry described in *The Rising* as a 'remarkably successful rampage through North Dublin and Meath', blowing up viaducts and railway lines, capturing RIC barracks and post offices, accumulating arms and ammunition and dismantling telephone and telegram lines.

On Friday morning, 28 April, at their base camp in an abandoned farmhouse just east of the main Dublin to Slane road, Ashe informed his section leaders that the day's objective was to destroy the Midland Great Western Railway line near Batterstown, in order to impede the progress of British reinforcements from Athlone. Three sections moved out, leaving the fourth, under Quartermaster Frank Lawless, to guard the camp and gather supplies. The convoy halted at Rath Cross, where Ashe issued orders to capture the RIC barracks about half a mile north of Ashbourne because, as Paul O'Brien explained in *Field of Fire: The Battle of Ashbourne, 1916*, it 'threatened the Volunteers' line of retreat from Batterstown'.

The commandant directed Section Leader Charlie Weston to position his men at the front of the barracks while the other two sections under Ned Rooney and Joseph Lawless were dispatched to cover the rear. As Volunteer Jerry Golden recalled in his BMH statement, a fusillade of rifle fire answered Ashe's demand to surrender the barracks 'in the name of the Irish Republic'. Ashe then gave the signal to attack. The ensuing firefight lasted for half an hour before a white cloth appeared through the window of the besieged barracks. While awaiting the emergence of the surrendering officers, the Volunteers heard the unmistakable sound of approaching motorcars. A convoy of twenty-four vehicles, carrying approximately sixty RIC reinforcements from Slane and Navan, was moving towards Rath Cross, just to the north of the barracks on the Slane road.

Making the most of the element of surprise, Weston's men moved quickly to take cover in the ditches and high banks overlooking the cross and opened fire on the approaching cars. The policemen emerged quickly, frantically seeking shelter before returning fire. 'It was at this point,' said Dr Richard Hayes in his BMH statement, that 'Mulcahy, in consultation with Ashe, began to show the tactical knowledge that was hours later to bring victory'.

The lieutenant ordered most of the Volunteers at the rear of the barracks to reinforce Weston's men at the cross and Ashe led the remaining seven Volunteers to a position at the rear left flank of the convoy before sending a runner for reinforcements. This strategic distribution of men and their rapid, systematic fire gave the illusion of a greater force. After hours of heavy fighting, the fourth section under Frank Lawless arrived with orders from Ashe to 'charge the police line from the Slane end'.

The column pushed forward, forcing the police towards the main body of Volunteers at the cross. The RIC men were surrounded. During a brief lull in the fighting, Jerry Golden saw about seven men charge down on the police with fixed bayonets: 'After about 10 minutes we heard the shout, "We Surrender."' With that the five hours of fighting ended.

Eileen Quinn recalled that among the heavy police casualties was fifty-eight-year-old County Inspector Alexander (Baby) Gray, who would have known her uncle when he served as district inspector in Dingle in 1887. She explained that 'Baby Gray was seriously wounded' and 'my uncle said, "Look, I know who you are. You know me, probably. Would you like help to heal your wounds?" Gray replied, "I would never take help from a Kerryman, least of all you."' Gray died of his wounds some twelve days later. Immortalised by Peig Sayers as an unsympathetic, uncompromising protagonist in her account of boycotting during the Land War, Gray's death at the hands of Ashe's men in 1916 brought symbolic closure to that chapter in local history.

The Volunteers returned to their camp in high spirits, but on Saturday news arrived of Pearse's surrender in Dublin. For Joseph Lawless, 'Pearse's signature was all too familiar [yet] … we could not accustom ourselves all at once to the idea that we, who were so far victorious in our fight, should surrender before we were attacked … This seemed to be the complete crashing of all our hopes.' The last body of rebels to surrender, and arguably the most successful, the Fingal Volunteers marched under military escort, according to Michael McAllister 'like near relatives at a funeral', the five miles to Swords for transport to Richmond Barracks.

As officer commanding the 5th Battalion, Ashe was court-martialled on 8 May 1916 and sentenced to death, but after a brief stay in Kilmainham Gaol, his sentence was commuted to penal servitude for life. He spent the next six months in Dartmoor Prison in Devon and was then moved to Lewes Prison in East Sussex, before his release in June 1917. In the aftermath of the Rising, 'The Battle of Ashbourne' passed into legend as a daring, well-organised Volunteer ambush of a larger, better-equipped enemy force, and Commandant Thomas Ashe emerged as an exemplary rebel leader.

More recently, commentators have suggested that the reality of the events that afternoon lies more in the realm of chaotic accident, with Ashe being demoted to the position of indecisive leader in favour of his more practical and steadfast second-in-command, Richard Mulcahy. This was certainly the opinion of Section Commander Joseph Lawless from Swords, who told his son, Colm, that 'Tom Ashe was very brave [but] when Dick Mulcahy arrived [on Monday evening] he actually took over as more of a military commander'.

In 1952 Nora Ashe took issue with suggestions by Lawless and by Desmond Ryan that her brother held only nominal command at Ashbourne. She insisted that the former had 'given the wrong impression on every occasion he has spoken of it' and the latter had 'not been fair to Tomás'. She claimed that Ashe 'had sent a dispatch to Lieutenant Mulcahy with instructions as to where to place his men and outlining his own position'. Eileen Quinn is similarly convinced that her uncle 'stayed in command out there'.

After his release in June 1917, Ashe, who had succeeded to the presidency of the Supreme Council of the IRB, resumed his political activities. Tall and handsome, with a commanding presence and a reputation as the only successful leader of the Rising, he travelled the country campaigning vigorously for Sinn Féin candidates in local by-elections and setting up corps of Volunteers.

Once Éamon de Valera achieved a decisive victory in East Clare, Ashe embarked on a speechmaking tour, making a particularity defiant address at Ballinalee in County Longford in July. He was arrested in Dublin in early September 1917, charged with 'causing disaffection among the civilian population' and sentenced to twelve months of hard labour in Mountjoy Prison. From

20 September the Kerryman led forty Sinn Féin prisoners in a hunger strike to demand political prisoner-of-war status and died five days later as a result of clumsily administered forcible feeding. In the words of fellow Kerryman and editor of the *Catholic Bulletin*, J. J. O'Kelly, 'The tragic death of Ashe moved the whole country to the deepest resentment and soon made more adherents to the republican cause.'

Around 30,000 mourners filed through City Hall where Ashe lay in state, and his funeral on 30 September was the largest in Dublin since that of Fenian Jeremiah O'Donovan Rossa two years before. Kevin O'Sheil recounted in his BMH statement how the city traffic was halted for hours as 'the vast procession moved through the thronged and reverently silent streets' of Dublin to Glasnevin Cemetery.

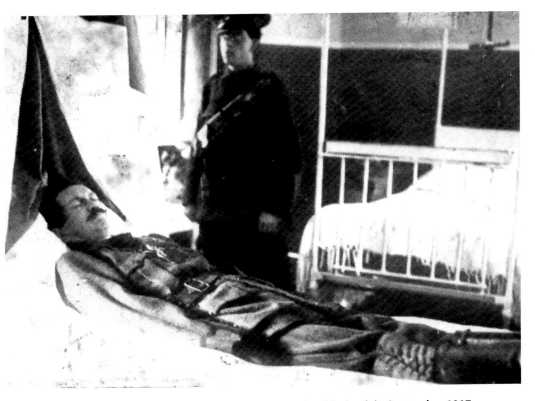

The body of Thomas Ashe, lying in repose, following his death in September 1917.

Eileen's mother, Bríd Clare from Rathfarnham, was among the thousands of spectators who watched Gregory Ashe march behind his son's coffin, followed by 700 armed and uniformed Kerry Volunteers. The Dublin Brigade turned out in force and Michael Collins, who succeeded Ashe as leader of the IRB, gave the graveside oration.

Eileen's father, Gregory, 'was working on the docks in New York' in September 1917 when he learned of his brother's death. His distress is evident in a letter written to his sister Nora on 3 October 1917:

> My heart is broken. I have not slept six hours in a week … I suppose Dada feels it terrible. I can't get him out of my mind because he will look at it in a different way to you … I dreamt of the house and Kinard during the nights [Thomas] was in the City Hall. I was never as lonesome as I was [looking] at the crowd from Lispole in Dublin.

Gregory returned to Ireland in late 1917 and after a short period in Dublin he 'went down to Lispole and got involved in the War of Independence'. He 'never spoke' to his family about his experiences as a member of the 5th Battalion, Kerry No. 1 Brigade during the War of Independence, or his internment in the Curragh during the Civil War, but his daughter suspects that his continued involvement in republican activities spoke to his anger and sense of responsibility for his brother's memory.

Gregory did not submit a witness testimony to the BMH. Like many anti-Treaty republicans, he was happier, Eileen explained, to relate his experiences to his friend Ernie O'Malley, who recorded these interviews in a series of notebooks now in the UCD Archives.

ASHE'S DEATH AND LEGACY

Ryle Dwyer

BEFORE Christmas 1916 all of those interned in Frongoch Internment Camp in Wales were freed. One of them, Michael Collins, on his return to Ireland, began reorganising the IRB and establishing an intelligence network. He managed to establish secret communications with the still incarcerated Thomas Ashe, who was considered the head of the IRB in the wake of the executions of the recognised leaders following the Rising.

In April 1917 Collins came up with a plan to nominate Joe McGuinness of Longford, one of the IRB men incarcerated in Lewes Prison, as a candidate for a forthcoming by-election in Longford. The plan was to highlight the continued imprisonment of these men by asking people to elect McGuinness as a means of demonstrating public support for the release of all the prisoners who took part in the Rising. Ashe was amenable to the plan, but Collins was overruled by Éamon de Valera and others, who feared McGuinness might be defeated and that this would set back the movement. 'Never allow yourselves to be beaten,' de Valera wrote from prison. 'Having started a fight see that you win. Act then with caution. Carefully size up the consequences of a projected action. If you feel that in the long run you can be beaten then don't begin.'

De Valera persuaded McGuinness to decline the candidacy, but the head-strong Collins would not stand for such timidity. Collins ignored the instructions he had received from Lewes and had McGuinness nominated anyway. The Big Fellow's judgment was vindicated when McGuinness was elected on the slogan: 'Put him in to get him out.' Thus, the electorate put him into parliament to get him out of jail.

The victory, which was announced on 10 May 1917, increased pressure on the British government to release the remaining prisoners. Within a month all the Irish prisoners were released, barely a year after Ashe, de Valera and others had been sentenced to life in prison.

At Lispole, Kinard and Dingle, bonfires blazed and huge crowds assembled to welcome home Ashe and the other West Kerry prisoners. Ashe spent only two days at home in Kinard before setting off around the country for a hectic series of speaking engagements. He spent some of his time in the Longford area, where he was courting Maud Kiernan, one of four sisters who were helping their brother Larry to run their family hotel, the Greville Arms, in Granard. On 5 August 1917 Ashe addressed a massive gathering at McKenna's Fort, near Banna, to mark the anniversary of Roger Casement's execution. Some 12,000 people thronged the area.

In late August Ashe was arrested and charged with making a seditious speech in Ballinalee, County Longford. Collins, who had shared the platform with him, visited him in prison and also attended his court martial a fortnight later. 'The whole business was extremely entertaining, almost as good a "Gilbert and

Thomas Ashe addressing a large gathering at McKenna's Fort near Banna Strand in August 1917, a year after Casement's execution. (Courtesy of Mercier Press)

Sullivan skit trial by jury"', Collins wrote to Ashe's sister Nora immediately afterwards. 'The President of the Court was obviously biased against Tom, and, although the charge is very trivial, and the witnesses contradicted each other, it is quite likely that Tom will be sentenced.'

Ashe was sentenced to two years' imprisonment with hard labour in Mountjoy Prison. Fourteen others were also convicted on similar charges, including his friend Austin Stack. They demanded prisoner-of-war status. When this was refused, they broke up the furniture in their cells. Ashe was then deprived of his bed, bedding and boots, and he protested by going on hunger strike. The authorities decided to force-feed him – a process whereby a tube was forcibly inserted into his nose, down through his throat and

Ashe speaks to an Irish Volunteer after delivering his address at Banna. (Courtesy of Mercier Press)

into his stomach and the food was then poured into the tube. On 25 September 1917, the fifth day of his hunger strike, Ashe suffered internal injuries during a force-feeding and died shortly after being moved to the Mater Hospital.

'If I die,' he said on his deathbed, 'I die in a good cause.'

Ashe's tragic death had a tremendous impact on the country. It provoked deep resentment and provided an even greater boost to republican recruitment than the executions following the Rising. His body, dressed in a Volunteer uniform, lay in state in the City Hall, Dublin.

Stack would probably have delivered the funeral oration, but he was in jail. Thus, Collins was selected. 'I grieve perhaps as no one else grieves,' Collins wrote at the time. In the uniform of a vice-commandant of the Volunteers, he delivered

Irish Volunteers firing party at the funeral of Thomas Ashe on 30 September 1917. (Courtesy of Mercier Press)

the graveside address after the last post was sounded and ceremonial shots were fired over the coffin. The oration was stirring in its simplicity. 'Nothing additional remains to be said … That volley which we have just heard is the only speech which it is proper to make over the grave of a dead Fenian.'

The cruel circumstances of Ashe's death resulted in an historic inquest. 'They have added another blood-spot to the Irish Calvary,' Tim Healy, who represented the Ashe family at the inquest, told the coroner's jury. He continued:

They have added bloody footprints on the road on which Irish martyrs have trodden. Have they gained by it? No. Other nations – not merely our own – will read with horror, and will set to the account to which properly it should belong, this terrible story of the death of Thomas Ashe. Other nations will read of it; and when they read it in time long yet to come, they will be enheartened and perhaps in their distress consoled, by the story of the uncomplaining martyrdom of this humble schoolmaster.

The jury concluded that Ashe's 'death was caused by the punishment of taking away from the cell bed, bedding and boots and allowing him to be on the cold floor for fifty hours, and then subjecting him to forcible feeding in his weak condition after hunger-striking for five or six days.' The British promptly capitulated on the other prisoners' demands for their own clothes, for the time being at least. 'Thomas Ashe is not dead,' Collins declared at a public gathering on 8 October in Ballinalee. 'His spirit is still with us.'

'I need no assurance that you and all our other friends throughout the country are delighted at our success in receiving better treatment,' Stack wrote from the prison the next day. 'All's well now – with the terrible exception of Ashe's loss – and we are in enjoyment of the treatment which we demanded for ourselves and for our fellow-countrymen.'

THE KERRYMAN'S EDITORIAL FOLLOWING THE DEATH OF THOMAS ASHE

Saturday 29 September 1917

So another name has been added to the long list of those glorious heroes who died that Ireland might live. Still one more of our countrymen has entered the Irish Valhalla to mingle with the Emmets, the Pearses and the Connollys. With those braves who have testified with their life-sacrifices to the indestructibility of Irish freedom.

'It is a sweet and glorious thing to die for one's country.' So it is – as much now as it was when the Roman spoke centuries ago. So believed Tom Ashe and he lived and died according to his belief.

But alas, alas that we should have learned that he is dead. 'Oh what glorious pride and sorrow fills the name of Ninety-Eight.' Thus goes the old ballad. Is it not the same now?

While we rejoice at the spirit of patriotism that fills the breast of those true sons of Erin who have so strikingly testified, within the past few years, to the overpowering love which the majority of Irishmen bear their motherland, we must weep beside the still open grave of Tom Ashe. . . .

During the Easter Week rising his valour and ability as a military commander were proved in a striking manner when in command of a small party of Irish Volunteers, he captured the survivors of a police force which exceeded Tom Ashe's little band by four to one.

He selflessly risked his life in open battle but Fate decreed that he should die in an English dungeon in Ireland.

And will the sacrifice which he has willingly rendered make his countrymen despondent or despairing?

No! On the contrary this latest victim to English system and regulations of Government will only make the people of Ireland more bitter and more determined to carry on the fight for the country's liberation.

O'RAHILLY'S LAST STAND

Ryle Dwyer

THE most senior member of the Irish Volunteers to be killed in the fighting of the Easter Rising was Michael Joseph O'Rahilly (1875–1916) of Ballylongford. It was, in a way, ironic, because he had been opposed to the Rising and had done his best to ensure that Eoin MacNeill's countermanding order was implemented.

Known widely as 'The O'Rahilly', he had been one of the driving forces in the formation of the Irish Volunteers in November 1913. He had been behind the IRB decision in Dublin to establish a military force, and it was believed that he was the inspiration behind MacNeill's formal call for the establishment of the Volunteers.

After the Larne gun-running by the Ulster Volunteers in April 1914, when a massive quantity of rifles and ammunition was successfully imported, O'Rahilly was heavily involved in the plans to arm the Irish Volunteers. As director of arms, he played a significant role in the gun-running at Howth on 26 July 1914.

When John Redmond, the leader of the IPP, issued his ultimatum to be allowed to pack the Volunteer executive

Michael 'The' O'Rahilly, director of arms for the Irish Volunteers in the build-up to the Rising. (Courtesy of Mercier Press)

committee with his own nominees, O'Rahilly was prepared to go along with it in order to keep the Volunteers in existence, as the withdrawal of Redmond's support at that juncture would have undermined the force. As later events were to show, the majority of the Volunteers were willing to follow Redmond's lead. Even Patrick Pearse, the most militant of the Volunteers, seemed to agree with O'Rahilly's reasoning. 'If the Parliamentarians help us to arm,' Pearse argued, 'it will be well worthwhile having surrendered to them.' But it turned out that Redmond's appointees did not have much influence, and the executive committee itself essentially lost its influence.

On 20 September 1914 Redmond threw his full support behind the British war effort by proclaiming at Woodenbridge, County Wicklow, that Ireland's duty was 'to the best of her ability to go wherever the firing line extends, in defence of right, of freedom, and religion in this war.' This was too much for O'Rahilly, who sent a four-word telegram to John Devoy, the IRB leader in the United States: 'Redmond's nominees fired out.'

By the beginning of 1916 the Volunteer executive was deeply divided, with Pearse, Éamonn Ceannt and Joseph M. Plunkett conspiring to use the Volunteers in a way opposed by MacNeill, that is to say, in an armed rebellion. They went so far as kidnapping a founding member and leading figure of the Irish Volunteers, Bulmer Hobson, just before Easter Week, to prevent him from influencing MacNeill against the Rising. On learning of the kidnapping, O'Rahilly went over to Pearse's school, St Enda's, and burst into Pearse's office, brandishing a revolver. 'Whoever kidnaps me will have to be a quicker shot!' he warned. Pearse placated him with an assurance that no harm would come to Hobson.

Although he supported MacNeill, O'Rahilly nevertheless did believe that a rebellion should be staged at some point while Britain was preoccupied with the war. He actually proclaimed in Athenry in December 1915 that he was 'praying for the chance to die for Ireland'.

The IRB had kept MacNeill, O'Rahilly and most of the others in the dark about their plans for Easter Week. MacNeill felt that such an action would be impractical and morally unjustifiable. Then, at the start of Holy Week 1916 Pearse informed MacNeill that he had documentary proof that Dublin Castle planned to round up the leadership of the Volunteers. MacNeill was persuaded to back the plans for the Rising on the assurance that the Germans were going to land weapons in Fenit. When he learned on Holy Saturday that the *Aud* had been scuttled and the weapons lost, this changed everything. He inserted a notice in the *Sunday Independent*:

> Owing to the very critical position, all orders given to Irish Volunteers for to-morrow, Easter Sunday, are hereby rescinded, and no parades, marches, or other movements of Irish Volunteers will take place. Each individual Volunteer will obey this order strictly in every particular.

He sent men around the country with orders cancelling all plans for the week-end. O'Rahilly, who was actually the last of the Volunteer leaders to learn of the rebellion plans, endorsed the idea of calling the whole thing off. He went off to Limerick to deliver the countermanding order personally. He arrived there at 5 a.m. on Easter Sunday, and Patrick Whelan was then sent on to Kerry with MacNeill's countermanding order.

After O'Rahilly got back to Dublin and had slept for a while, Desmond Fitz-Gerald – an English-born Irish nationalist and one of the more active Volunteer organisers – informed him that Pearse and the others had reset the Rising to begin around noon the following day, Easter Monday. O'Rahilly said, 'If the men I have trained to fight are going into action, I must be with them.'

Many were surprised when O'Rahilly turned up in a motorcar outside Liberty Hall as they were forming up to march on the General Post Office (GPO). He loaded his car with materiel and drove to the back of the GPO, where the stuff was unloaded. He then took charge of the upper part of the GPO during the Rising.

After the order was given to abandon the burning GPO on Friday, O'Rahilly turned to Fr J. Flanagan and asked for his blessing and absolution. 'We shall never meet in this world again, Father,' he said. He knew that in all likelihood he was charging out of the building to his death. Here was his chance to fulfil his wish 'to die for Ireland'.

Before leaving the GPO he turned to his men. 'It will be either a glorious victory or a glorious death, boys,' he said. He then led them into Moore Street, where he was quickly cut down by machine-gun fire. Many people recalled seeing his body as it lay by the side of the road, but it seemed that he was not clinically dead. Almost twenty hours later, when the British were clearing up the scene, one of the men remarked that O'Rahilly was still alive. 'That's a Sinn Féin officer,' one of the British officers snapped, as he ordered the man to leave him. 'The more of them that die naturally, the fewer we'll have to shoot.'

O'RAHILLY'S LIFE AND FAMILY

Hélène O'Keeffe

FORTY-ONE-YEAR-OLD Michael Joseph O'Rahilly, one of the founding members of the Volunteers, was chosen to lead an advance party of twenty-five Volunteers in the evacuation from the GPO on Friday 28 April 1916. Their desperate mission, conceived in chaos, was to mount a frontal attack on the British barricade at the intersection of Moore Street and Parnell Street, in an attempt to distract the British military long enough for the rest of the garrison to escape the blazing GPO.

At around 7.30 p.m. they emerged from the side entrance of the shell-damaged building into Henry Place. The small party rushed for the corner of Henry Street, turned right into Moore Street and into the sights of the machine guns of the 6th Sherwood Foresters at the barricade at the end of the street. The first volley cut through their ranks. They scattered, frantically seeking shelter in the narrow doorways on both sides of the street.

O'Rahilly made it to within thirty yards of the barricade and swerved into a doorway at the corner of Sampson's Lane. When the shooting subsided, he blew twice on his whistle, signalling to his men to advance, and with a Mauser pistol in one hand and a sword in the other, he dashed out into the middle of Moore Street. He covered only a short distance before he was cut down. He lay motionless for a few seconds before painfully dragging himself the short distance into Sackville Lane. Aware of his inevitable fate, he reached into his pocket to retrieve the note that had been sent to the GPO on Wednesday by his eleven-year-old son, Aodogán. It read: 'Dear Dada … I heard from Nell and Anna that the Volunteers are winning. I don't suppose they will ever get the GPO for as long as you are in command.'

On the reverse of the crumpled page, O'Rahilly penned his last words to his family:

Written after I was shot. Darling Nancy I was shot leading a rush up Moore Street, took refuge in a doorway. While I was there I heard the men pointing out where I was and I made a bolt for the lane I am in now. I got more [than] one bullet I think. Tons and tons of love dearie to you and the boys and to Nell and Anna. It was a good fight anyhow. Please deliver this to Nannie O'Rahilly, 40 Herbert Park, Dublin. Goodbye darling.

Proinsias Ó Rathaille finds it difficult to discuss the suffering and indignity of his grandfather's prolonged death, but has always been moved by the pathos of his final act:

There were two holes in the note from the Maxim machine gun on Parnell Square … and the blood was flowing down his hand when he was writing it. As far as I remember, he just folded the note and managed [to] put it back in his pocket and [then] … he wrote on the wall with his finger covered in blood: 'The O'Rahilly died here' … He was a brave man.

O'Rahilly was born on 22 April 1875 in a house at the corner of Bridge Street and Quay Street in Ballylongford. When his father died in 1896, the young medical student abandoned his studies in University College Dublin to manage the lucrative family business in Kerry. Three years later he married Philadelphia-born Nancy (Nannie) Brown and, after a series of different addresses in Ireland and the United States, the couple and their four young sons settled at 40 Herbert Park in Ballsbridge in Dublin. By this time he was well read, well travelled, reasonably wealthy and a generous donor to the nationalist cause which he espoused.

After his repatriation in 1909, O'Rahilly revived an old association with Arthur Griffith, founder of Sinn Féin and editor of nationalist newspaper the *United Irishman*. In 1910 he joined the executive of Sinn Féin and from 1911 he sat on the Gaelic League's governing body (An Coiste Gnótha).

It was in Ventry on the Dingle peninsula – where he had a holiday cottage – that he established a formative friendship with Desmond FitzGerald, who later, in an *Irish Times* article entitled 'Inside the GPO' published on 7 April 1966, recalled the 'carefree days when we shared our love of the beautiful countryside of Kerry and our dreams of a new and heroic spirit of Irish nationalism that was about to come into being'.

While not a member of the secretive oath-bound IRB, O'Rahilly advocated militancy in the name of Irish independence and on 20 January 1913 he seconded Éamonn Ceannt's motion to the national council of Sinn Féin that 'it was the duty of all Irishmen to possess knowledge of arms'. Both these men were also among the small group that gathered in Wynn's Hotel in Dublin on 11 November to discuss the formation of an Irish Volunteer movement.

A founding member of the Irish Aero Club, O'Rahilly had an ardent interest in 'mechanical things', and in 1911 he bought a beautiful, green De Dion-Bouton car which, in Proinsias's words, he used 'to ferry all the guns in from the *Asgard*' after it landed at Howth on 26 July 1914.

O'Rahilly and his automobile were called to service once more on Saturday 22 April 1916 when, as Proinsias explained, 'Eoin MacNeill asked my grandfather would he drive down to Limerick to cancel the Rising'. Like MacNeill, O'Rahilly was appalled when he learned about the loss of the *Aud* and denounced the planned rebellion as inopportune and premature. His grandson continued:

> When he came back in his car [on Sunday afternoon] the heat and the steam was coming out of it in front of Herbert Park. He was a very tired man and he went to bed [but] was awoken by Desmond FitzGerald [who said,] 'It's started, you'll have to come into town to the GPO.' He was wiping the sleep from his eyes and he just said, 'Well I suppose I've wound up the clock, I better go in and hear it strike.' So he kissed his wife goodbye, said goodbye to the kids and drove in, and … as they say, the rest is history.

Proinsias added:

Having abandoned his *gluaisteán* outside the GPO, The O'Rahilly received a guarded reception from the Volunteers inside who knew that he considered the Rising 'a glorious madness'. He quickly regained their confidence as a commanding presence in the rebel headquarters and took over as treasurer. He emptied all the cash [from the tills] and put it into one safe and he was the only key-holder apparently.

O'Rahilly also took responsibility for the safety of the prisoners. Cumann na mBan member Min Ryan remembered the instruction that he gave: '"If it's the last bit of food in the place, it must be shared with the prisoners and if any man does not follow my instructions he will get this" – and he pulled out his gun.' In the context of his grandfather's 'careful and decent' treatment of his prisoners, Proinsias found it even more 'hurtful' that 'the British wouldn't let anyone near

The remains of O'Rahilly's cherished car outside the GPO.
(Courtesy of Mercier Press)

his body as he lay fatally wounded'. He also despaired at the ignominious theft of O'Rahilly's rings and watch while he lay dying in a doorway.

For Desmond FitzGerald, O'Rahilly was 'the most tragic figure in that tragic gathering of men' because 'he was devoted to his wife and family with a rare devotion, but he had decided to leave them to serve Ireland when the call to service came'. It was small consolation for his wife, who was six months pregnant with their fifth child.

Proinsias knows that his grandmother, whom he remembers as 'quiet and very elegant', was heartbroken at the news. The children were 'devastated that they had lost their father so young', but, Proinsias insists, 'my father always [considered it] the ultimate gesture'. Proinsias's uncle Aodogán O'Rahilly echoed this sentiment on 4 April 1991, when he told *The Irish Times*: 'One of my brothers used to say that it was irresponsible for a man to go out and leave his wife and four young children. And go into a fight in which he was going to get killed. I never felt that. I felt that he did what had to be done … [He was] a heroic figure.'

FIONÁN LYNCH

Hélène O'Keeffe

ON 24 April 1916, uniformed and armed with Lee Enfield rifles and Howth Mausers, fifty men of the 1st Battalion, Dublin Brigade, paraded at the Gaelic League Hall in Blackhall Street in Dublin. Their commandant, Edward Daly, declared that this 'was the day' and instructed his officers to lead their six companies, depleted by confusion and countermand, to their designated locations in the Four Courts area on the north side of the Liffey.

Captain Fionán Lynch (1889–1966) marched at the head of 'F' Company towards what was to become one of the most hotly contested battlegrounds of the Rising. According to his youngest son, Dr Gearóid Lynch, the veteran sometimes spoke about the events of Easter Week, but 'in a quiet way … he never had any joy in it. I think he found [the memory] distressing at times but it didn't spoil his life. He was a very contained man.'

Fionán Lynch was born on 17 March 1889 in Kilmackerrin, Cahersiveen to the 'founding schoolmaster and schoolmistress' of the local national school. His parents provided his early education, after which he attended Rockwell and Blackrock Colleges and St Patrick's College in Drumcondra. He lived briefly in Swansea in South Wales before returning to Dublin in April 1912 to take up a teaching position at St Michan's National School in Halston Street. Not long afterwards, Seán Mac Diarmada recruited the native Irish speaker into the IRB. Lynch shared 'digs' at 44 Mountjoy Street with fellow teacher and 'very close friend' Gearóid O'Sullivan.

In 1912 both men became enthusiastic members of the influential Keating Branch of the Gaelic League, and in November of the following year they were among the first to enrol in the Irish Volunteers. Lynch, in his BMH statement, described his life in those days as 'being very full indeed'. He and O'Sullivan combined their work as teachers with their duties as Volunteers, active members of the Gaelic League and co-founders of Piaras Béaslaí's Irish-language dramatic society, Na hAisteori.

Lynch's responsibilities increased in the summer of 1914 when he was elected captain of 'F' Company, 1st Battalion. However, he was forced to sever his connection with the Volunteers in early 1916, when the manager of his school threatened to withdraw his salary. He left with the assurance that if there were 'anything doing' he would return to lead them. The officers in attendance at a meeting of the battalion council in April were left in no doubt that a rebellion was imminent and on Holy Thursday Lynch formally resumed command of 'F' Company. As he recounted in his BMH statement: 'I reminded the men of what I had told them a few months before when leaving them – that when there would be "anything doing" I would be back to lead them. I then said "Well, I am back" and I will ever remember with pride the cheers with which that announcement was greeted.'

In the days before the Rising, when tensions were 'at fever-height', Lynch's men were assigned guard duty for the protection of the members of the Volunteer executive. Seán Mac Diarmada took up temporary residence with Lynch and O'Sullivan at 44 Mountjoy Street, where, early on Saturday 22 April, he received word of Casement's arrest in Kerry. Lynch was immediately dispatched to St Enda's College to escort Patrick Pearse to a crisis meeting of the Military Council, the seven-man subcommittee of the IRB Supreme Council formed to plan and organise the Rising, at Liberty Hall. Confusion and frustration followed in the wake of MacNeill's countermanding order on Sunday but, after a prolonged meeting at the Keating Branch of the Gaelic League in North Frederick Street, the Military Council resolved to proceed with the Rising at midday on Easter Monday.

On that day, armed with the rifle retrieved from its hiding place at 44 Mountjoy Street, twenty-seven-year-old Lynch led his men towards their pre-allocated positions in Church Street and North King Street. On their captain's instructions they began building barricades with timber, 'bits of old furniture' and 'a lot of stuff out of yards'. Other than negotiations with opportunistic looters and antagonistic local residents, 'F' Company saw little action until Wednesday. However, from that point until the surrender on Saturday Lynch's men were locked in 'intense' combat with a battalion of the South Staffordshire Regiment.

North King Street in particular became the focus of vicious street fighting, as a small garrison of twenty men under Lieutenant Jack Shouldice struggled to hold their strategic position in Reilly's public house against the British forces. The Volunteers repulsed attack after attack on Friday, so in the early hours of Saturday morning Lieutenant Colonel Henry Taylor ordered his soldiers to begin tunnelling through the interior walls of the houses in North King Street towards 'Reilly's Fort'.

Progress was slow and at dawn an impatient Taylor ordered his men to charge the rebel stronghold with bayonets fixed. The British platoon ran into a wall of bullets fired from several directions. They lost nine men and many more were wounded. During an interview with BBC radio in 1964, Lynch said, 'It was, of course, a tragic thing in many ways. One had to be sorry for them; they were only very young boys and, in fact, Lieutenant Shouldice told me that when he went to collect the rifles with others, he heard one lad saying, "Oh Mammy, Mammy", which was terrible.'

Lynch also remembered the Volunteer casualties. On Saturday morning, crouched at a barricade near the junction of Church Street and Nicholas Avenue, he watched as Cork Volunteer Seán Hurley was struck in the head by a bullet fired from a British armoured car. 'We got him into the hall of a house and got word over the roofs to the priests next door that he was dying and then scrambled over the roofs ourselves and into May Lane … and out of range of the armoured car. Then we fell back onto the Four Courts.'

On Saturday evening Commandant Daly received the order to surrender and the Four Courts garrison was marched to the small green outside the Rotunda Gardens. The next morning they were escorted under military guard through the desolate city to Richmond Barracks in Inchicore.

After his court martial on 4 May Lynch was transferred to Kilmainham Gaol, where, as his son explained, he endured the prolonged agony of awaiting his sentence. 'Every night he heard the tramp, tramp, tramp of boots and about four [men] at a time would be told that they were to be executed in the morning. Eventually his turn came and the soldiers on duty walked in. He was ordered to stand up. Then he was told that his sentence of death had been commuted to ten years' penal servitude.'

Lynch spent a brief period in Mountjoy Prison, where, much to the amusement of the 'stout warder', his cell door was incorrectly labelled 'Fenian Lynch'. He was subsequently transported to Portland Prison on the Isle of Wight before finally being sent to Frongoch Internment Camp in Wales. Released in the general amnesty of December 1916, Lynch was rearrested for 'seditious speechmaking' in May 1917 and imprisoned once again in Mountjoy. While there, he took part in a hunger strike with fellow Kerrymen Austin Stack and Thomas Ashe to demand prisoner-of-war status. Lynch claimed to have been the last to speak to Ashe before his death. 'They exchanged words through the bars as he went by,' Gearóid explained. 'It affected him deeply.'

Lynch offered his recollections to the BBC in 1964:

We resisted all the time … We refused to move from our cells to the places where they used to forcibly feed [us] so we had to be carried bodily. [This went on for days] and we used to shout out to each other 'Stick it.' On 27 September 1917, as Ashe was being carried away, I said, 'Stick it, Tom Boy', and Ashe said, 'I'll stick it Fin.' I saw him come back about a quarter of an hour or ten minutes later absolutely blue in the face and I knew that something serious had happened.

Lynch was released from Mountjoy Prison in November 1917. However, as an anti-conscription activist, he was one of more than seventy members of Sinn Féin arrested in May 1918 as part of the German Plot, an alleged conspiracy between Sinn Féin and the German Empire to start another armed insurrection in Ireland. In December, while still in custody, he was elected unopposed as Sinn

Féin TD for South Kerry. He was eventually released from prison in August 1919 and the following November married Bridget Slattery from Tralee, with whom he had six sons and a daughter.

In 1921 Lynch served as assistant secretary to the Treaty delegation. 'My mother went [to London] as well,' Gearóid said. The ladies 'went to be hostesses to any function they were involved in' and 'they were [also] typists and secretaries'.

A strong supporter of the Anglo-Irish Treaty, Lynch went on to serve in both the Provisional Government and the National Army during the Civil War. He was Minister for Fisheries in the fraught early years of the Free State, when, according to his son, 'he slept every night with a revolver under the pillow'. In conversation about how his father dealt with Civil War bitterness, Gearóid said: 'He was a very gentle person and when the awkward things came up he'd say, "Ah, forget it. It's history."'

Fionán Lynch, the only TD to be elected to and serve in every Dáil from 1918 to 1944, retired from politics to enter the legal profession and was eventually appointed a circuit court judge. He died suddenly in June 1966, shortly after the fiftieth anniversary commemorations of the 1916 Rising.

PATRICK O'CONNOR

Hélène O'Keeffe

ON Friday 28 April 1916 Kerry Volunteer Patrick O'Connor (1882–1916) surveyed the scene inside the smoke-filled GPO. British artillery shook the very foundations of the post office where, less than a week before, he had worked as a sorter. The Volunteers scrambled to quench the raging fires as debris crashed around them, and a hastily convened council of war determined that their only option was to evacuate. O'Connor was among the twenty-five men who answered Michael J. O'Rahilly's call for Volunteers to lead an advance guard. They emerged into Henry Place around 7.30 p.m. and less than half an hour later, the Volunteer from Rathmore lay mortally wounded on Moore Street.

O'Connor grew up with his six siblings on what his niece Kitty Murphy called a 'reasonably good farm'. Kitty's father, Daniel O'Connor, was disinclined to speak about his brother, but Kitty's mother, Annie O'Leary, told her 'occasional things that a man wouldn't'. She learned, for example, that even though things were 'quite lively' in Rathmore when Patrick was a young man, he 'was not a person for socialising'.

> Maybe my father wouldn't talk about how distant he found him or how unfriendly because they were all the one family. But my mother said he might come visiting and if you talked about political things he was geared up but [otherwise he] didn't talk. He was a very distant, silent person [and] he rarely laughed. He never had a girl, he never went dancing; all he wanted was history and to be involved in something. His brother Denis, on the other hand, was totally different and had girls all over the place. He was an accordion player and he played for every house dance that was around the place.

Patrick's mother, Mary O'Donoghue from Glenflesk, had a significant radicalising influence on her 'serious' son. She had lived through the Great Famine in the 1840s and 'remembered the people cutting the nettles and taking them home to … keep them from the hunger'. She often told Patrick about what she considered 'the cruelty of the English that time'.

He was also inspired by Irish-Ireland propaganda and the gospel of self-reliance preached in the pages of Arthur Griffith's *United Irishman*. He refused to buy anything other than Irish-manufactured goods and 'one time he walked ten kilometres to Barraduff to buy a box of Irish matches'. He was also 'an intellectual', Kitty explained, and 'came first in Ireland, England and Scotland in his civil service exam'.

At eighteen years of age Patrick left his native Kerry to take a position as a sorter in the Post Office in London. 'It so happened that the people he was working with were very involved in Gaelic things' and 'then he got transferred to the GPO in Dublin in 1915 and, of course, he got very much involved there again'. He joined 'F' Company, 1st Battalion, Dublin Brigade of the Irish Volunteers and found lodgings with Cork Volunteer Seán Hayes at 77 Heytesbury Street.

According to his mother's pension application in 1924, Patrick was 'the first man of his company to purchase a rifle'. He was also Mary O'Connor's 'chief means of support', sending her half of his wages every week and visiting her in Rathmore whenever he could. On one such visit in early 1916, local Volunteer leader Daniel Dennehy inducted O'Connor into the IRB.

Patrick returned to Kerry for the last time on Holy Wednesday 1916. Kitty explained:

His father and his brother died within seven days of each other and he came down from Dublin for the funerals. His brother Denis was only about thirty-six, I'd say. He was an athlete and he ran in a race over in London. The heavens opened and he got all wet and he left on the wet clothes [when] he [went out] to celebrate that night. He developed TB and he died of it. He was buried on the Good Friday and his father was buried on the Tuesday or the Wednesday before that.

In the meantime, the local Volunteers prepared for the march to Tralee on Easter Sunday. Dan Dennehy, captain of the Rathmore Company, told the BMH that, as he 'knew what was coming', he implored Patrick on Good Friday to fight with the Rathmore men. Patrick, however, insisted on returning to the capital and departed for the train station 'in good spirits and anxious for the fight'.

O'Connor joined the GPO garrison on Monday. On Tuesday he helped to establish lines of communication from Volunteer headquarters. On Wednesday he assisted in the futile attempts to put out the raging fires in Tyler's, Clerys and the adjoining buildings. Two days later he was mortally wounded in a hail of machine-gun fire from the British barricade at the junction of Moore Street and Parnell Street. Limerick Volunteer Éamonn T. Dore testified in his BMH statement that 'my nearest comrade, Pat O'Connor, was killed just in front of me and falling on me pinned me under him'.

Mary O'Connor was unwilling to send anyone up to Dublin 'until everything had settled down quiet' and Kitty regrets that the family missed an opportunity to speak to the people who might 'have given them the story from the start'. They only had 'second-hand information'. Notwithstanding Dore's testimony, Kitty feels that the most authentic version of events is that Patrick 'was shot in Moore Street', but 'he was not dead at the time they removed his body and he later died in hospital'. They were able to identify him because 'he got a poisoned finger [which] had to be amputated and one nurse said that she attended to a dying man who had only three-quarters of his index finger'.

Patrick's brothers avoided active involvement in the struggle for independence after 1916. 'They all had children that time,' Kitty explained, 'and I suppose for their mother's sake they didn't do any more.' Nonetheless, the family 'were marked people all their lives'. Daniel told his daughter that 'they used to all gather around at night … afraid that they could be raided or shot on account of [Patrick] taking such an active part. They were living in fear.'

In 1924 Mary told the Army Pensions Committee that the Black and Tans and the local RIC had burned her house and her belongings 'for no reason [other than] Paddy's action in the past'. The raids were also based on intelligence that the O'Connor farm was a safe house for members of the local flying column. Kitty remembered hearing about 'a great woman down in the Bridge Bar' who would alert the family if she heard about a potential raid, and would 'tell my father and mother don't keep anybody tonight'.

Born on 6 September 1922, 'at the very end' of the troubles, Kitty was able to relate little else about her family's involvements in the 1916–23 period. 'You see my father and mother had suffered so much that I think they would rather have forgotten it.'

MIKE KNIGHTLY

Ryle Dwyer

MIKE Knightly (1888–1965) was from Ballyard, Tralee. He went to work for the *Irish Independent* in Dublin in 1913, and was active in the 1st Battalion of the Irish Volunteers in the city, in a company under the command of Fionán Lynch.

On Easter Monday 1916 Knightly reported for work at the *Irish Independent* offices, but on learning of the seizure of the GPO, he went there later that day to offer his services. When he knocked on the main door, it was Michael O'Rahilly who opened it and invited him into the building, once his identity had been confirmed by Seán Mac Diarmada.

Knightly served most of his time in the GPO on the ground floor, where he observed some of the leaders. 'James Connolly … appeared to be the most active of the senior officers,' Knightly wrote in his BMH statement about 1916.'He struck me as being a man of exceptionally forcible character. I thought what a great general he would make in more favourable circumstances.'

After the Rising, Knightly was initially kept in Richmond Barracks and then transferred to Wakefield Prison and finally Frongoch Internment Camp. Throughout the War of Independence he continued to work as a journalist, using his position to provide useful information to the IRA and Sinn Féin. During the Treaty negotiations he served as a press officer with the Irish delegation in London.

Knightly went on to become chief editor of the Oireachtas debates until the start of the Second World War, when he became chief newspaper censor. Afterwards he returned to his Oireachtas post, where he remained until his retirement in 1955.

J. J. McELLIGOTT

Ryle Dwyer

J. J. (James John) McElligott (1893–1974) grew up in Castle Street, Tralee, where his parents owned a shop and bar. He served in the GPO during the Rising and during the fighting he was one of three men who brought food, under heavy fire, to colleagues on the other side of Sackville Street (now O'Connell Street). Throughout the week McElligott spent much of his time on the rooftop of the GPO, before fire forced the Volunteers to abandon the building.

Following the evacuation of the GPO, when a group was ordered to attack a suspected enemy sniper's nest in a house in Moore Street, McElligott charged in on his own. He kicked in the front door, and then, carrying his rifle, searched each room, only to find that there was nobody else in the building. 'I didn't feel a bit heroic,' he later explained. 'I was roaring like the bull of Bashan and simply mad, mad, mad.'

He was later deported to Stafford Prison, where he was in the cell next to Michael Collins. While Collins and most of the others were interned at Frongoch in Wales, McElligott was freed and returned to Ireland. He was the most senior crown civil servant dismissed for participating in the Rising.

McElligott did not leave a witness statement with the BMH about his involvement in the Rising, which may have something to do with the fact that he had claimed after the Rising that he had been forced into the GPO. He said that he had just returned from the Fairyhouse race meeting on that Easter Monday when he bumped into some Volunteer colleagues who compelled him to take part in the Rising.

He later distinguished himself as one of the foremost civil servants in Ireland's history. When people write about the most effective Irish civil servants they inevitably consider T. K. Whitaker, John Leydon and the Moynihan brothers, Maurice and Seán; it should be remembered, however, that those four came to prominence serving under McElligott in the Department of Finance.

MICHAEL MULVIHILL

Hélène O'Keeffe

IN December 1966 Michael Mulvihill's sixty-three-year-old sister Margaret attended the ceremonial unveiling of a plaque in his honour at their homestead in Ardoughter, Ballyduff. The tribute to the fallen rebel was little comfort to his sister, who was profoundly bitter about what she perceived as a lack of respect shown by the government to the families of the men who had given their lives 'gloriously' in 1916. Her grand-nephew Liam Hutchinson, who spent his childhood summers with the 'remnants of the Mulvihill family' in Kerry, is more conscious of their material sacrifices than he is of his grand-uncle's 'patriotic sacrifice'.

Described by his nephew – also called Michael – in the Mulvihill clan newsletter, *The Mulvihill Voice*, as 'an athletic man … with a scholarly face and penetrating eyes', eighteen-year-old Michael Mulvihill (1879–1916) left home in 1897 in search of employment in London. He secured a job as 'a sorter in the Post Office' at £295 per annum, £2 of which he sent home to Ardoughter every week. The money was essential to his parents and eight siblings, who subsisted on a meagre pension.

In 1903 Michael's father, John, had retired 'prematurely' from his job as the principal of Ballincrossig National School after a series of disputes with the school clerical manager about the appropriateness of 'Fenianism' in the classroom. This 'left the family in very poor and straitened circumstances', Liam Hutchinson explains. He recalls that Margaret and Tom Mulvihill were 'tremendously proud of their brother, and with good reason. He gave his life in the GPO for which we should all be thankful, in my opinion.' But Michael's 'dedication to his family's survival' was, in Liam's opinion, just as noble as his dedication to his county. 'If it hadn't been for Mike, they would have finished up in the workhouse or somewhere … He helped them [to] survive and made sure that his [siblings] were well educated.'

'A renowned hurler' and 'fluent Irish speaker', Michael became an active member of the GAA and the Gaelic League in London and was sworn into the IRB shortly after his arrival in the city. His grand-nephew suggests that Michael's radicalism was born during his childhood in Kerry in the 1880s:'It was only a few short years since we had that awful famine and there is no question that the people who managed to survive the traumatic experience … held this tremendous bitterness.'

Liam feels that 'there is every reason to believe' that his own grandfather, John Mulvihill,'was an IRB man as well'. He 'spent a lot of time travelling over and back to America … but he was a man of mystery like an awful lot of the men at that time were'.

Michael formed close associations with 'most of the prominent nationalists in London' and, in 1913, he and his brother-in-law, Austin Kennan from Dublin, were among the 'founding members' of the London Corps of the Irish Volunteers.

Three years later, on 5 January 1916, the British government introduced the first in a series of Military Service Acts, which initiated conscription to the British Army and, shortly before Easter, thirty-seven-year-old Michael was called up for military service. According to Austin Kennan, in an article published in *The Kerryman* on 19 November 1966:

> He ignored the call, thus forfeiting his civil service post and becoming a wanted man liable to arrest anywhere in Britain or Ireland. He discussed with me the strong rumours of an early insurrection and we decided to go to Dublin. We did this on Good Friday, accompanied by Seán McGrath who carried a gun in a travelling rug.

Kennan also recounted how:

> the three of us stayed at the Kincora Hotel in Parnell Square [and] Mick signed his name as 'O'Connor' [his mother's maiden name] for the benefit of any DMP [Dublin

Metropolitan Police] men who might inspect the register. We knew that certain members of that force were making a speciality of tracing Irishmen who left Britain rather than join the British Army.

The London exiles arrived in Larkfield, Kimmage, on Saturday and were disappointed to find that George Plunkett had 'no definite news about a rising'. They returned to the city, and on Easter Monday were delighted to learn that the rebels had taken the GPO. Kennan and Mulvihill came within sight of the rebel headquarters just as the Kimmage garrison marched into Sackville Street. Kennan recalled that London Volunteer 'Denis Daly from Kerry, waved to us and said, "This is revolution!" We entered the Post Office and Mick and I were given shot guns and a quantity of bombs … and the two of us took up position on the front of the roof near the centre.' Mulvihill and Kennan, together with members of the Kimmage garrison and the Rathfarnham Company of St Enda's students, exchanged fire with the British forces. Kennan recorded that they were visited on the roof by Patrick Pearse and Michael Collins, 'with whom [they] had been closely associated in London' and by 'a priest who gave [them] general absolution'.

On Thursday, when the British bombardment of the rebel positions around the GPO intensified, Mulvihill and Kennan were ordered to the ground floor and posted to new positions at the windows to prepare for the expected frontal assault. That night, Sackville Street was set alight by incendiary shells, and the wholesale destruction of the most beautiful street in Ireland was an awesome and terrifying spectacle. 'Not a soul was now to be seen,' reported Rathfarnham Volunteer Feargus de Burca in his BMH statement, 'only a huge wall of flames towering to the sky and great billows of smoke. The noise of bursting shells and tumbling walls and roofs was indescribable.'

The shelling of Sackville Street continued on Friday and after the first direct hit, at 3 p.m., the upper floors of the GPO were quickly engulfed by fire. It became clear that withdrawal was inevitable. Kennan searched unsuccessfully for his brother-in-law amid the chaos of the evacuation and later learned that Mulvihill had volunteered with fellow Kerrymen Denis Daly, Patrick O'Connor and Patrick Shortis to join Michael O'Rahilly's vanguard. They had dashed forward to Henry Place and around the corner into Moore Street and the sights of the British machine guns.

On 14 March 1947 Margaret Mulvihill stitched together in a letter to a J. Lyons in Cork the various threads of truth and conjecture about her brother's death and concluded that 'his body, until buried by the military authorities, laid stretched, dead, face downwards in Moore Lane at the junction of Henry Place'.

Michael's death 'devastated' his family in Ardoughter, and his grand-nephew was 'not surprised' to hear that the 'independently minded' John Mulvihill refused assistance from the White Cross, despite the fact that the family had been so dependent on his son's financial assistance. Apparently, 'old John Mulvihill' said: 'We never took money for killing people and we are certainly not taking money for being killed.'

John died in June 1923 and a month later his widow, Mary, made an application for a Dependants' Allowance under the newly enacted Army Pensions Act. By May 1924 she was becoming increasingly anxious about 'the undue delay in dealing with [her] claim', as she explained in a letter to the adjutant general, because, at seventy-one, she was supporting her 'invalid' son Thomas and daughter Margaret, who was in 'ill health, suffering from the effects of acute pleurisy contracted some years before'. She asked why she was being allowed to starve by the government of the country for which her son fought and died.

Eventually the claim was approved, but when Mary Mulvihill died in 1944 the payment of the vital allowance of £1 per week was terminated. In 1947 her daughter Margaret, 'destitute and extremely worried', was moved to invoke her brother's memory in a letter to the *Irish Press* columnist P. J. Lyons on behalf of her brother Thomas, who, at forty-seven, was passed over for civil service employment in the Department of Industry and Commerce in favour of 'ex-army men'. She wrote with bitter sarcasm: 'All I can say is that we got great thanks from the Government for Michael's patriotism.'

Two years later, when the family received an 'ejectment order' for non-payment of council rates, Margaret made an emotional appeal to local Labour Party TD Dan Spring to lobby on her behalf for the allowance to be reinstated in her name. Unsuccessful in 1949, Margaret wrote again in August 1953 to the secretary of the Department of Defence, claiming to be 'in dire circumstances'. Based on the provisions of that year's amendment to the Military Service Pensions Act, she asked for a 'special allowance in respect of the death and services of my brother Michael Mulvihill … who was gloriously killed in action in the GPO on Easter Sunday [sic] 1916'. She was finally successful, but her long struggle with penury bred a deep resentment towards the institutions of the state for which her brother had 'sacrificed his life'.

This resentment was evident in the Golden Jubilee year when she declined Seán Lemass's invitation to attend a commemorative ceremony in Arbour Hill. Writing to Tom McEllistrim, TD, in March 1966, she explained:

> I think now that all this is for the leaders' relatives or the Queen Bees of the Rising … Miss Pearse etc., are the only ones to be treated by any Government we have had. Yet, in a quiet way, Michael brought in more arms each year than any of these … He got the death he wished and we could not stop him but I think now, like [Daniel] O'Connell, that any country is not worth a drop of human blood.

The Kerry Volunteers bequeathed a legacy of loss and a material burden on their families, but their names also carried a political weight that propelled their brothers and sisters into the midst of conflict during the War of Independence and the Civil War.

Even though 'nobody was turned away from the Mulvihill home in Ardough-ter', the family was not actively engaged in the War of Independence. Michael's youngest brother, Tom, felt that 'the substantial contribution of his family was completed in 1916'. Despite his abstention, Tom was 'badly beaten' by the Black and Tans, who, according to his grand-nephew, 'had a habit of going back to families that had participated [in the Rising] and giving them some special treatment'. He received 'very bad chest injuries and always had breathing difficulties [and] was never really fit for full-time work after that'.

Liam regrets that during his youth he did not ask his grand-uncle 'more pertinent questions', but feels that even if he had, he would have found Thomas was from a generation 'that was quite reticent' about talking about what happened: 'I suppose they saw some terrible things and maybe they just wanted to leave it behind.'

Michael Mulvihill is buried with Patrick O'Connor and Patrick Shortis in the Republican Plot in St Paul's Cemetery in Glasnevin, Dublin. 'The grave was unmarked for a number of years,' Liam explained, 'but in 1929 the National Graves Association cordoned off the area and put up a headstone.' This was replaced in 1966 with a monument on which is inscribed a line from W. B. Yeats's poem 'Easter 1916': 'We know their dream ... they dreamed and are dead'.

PATRICK SHORTIS

Hélène O'Keeffe

IN the autumn of 1911 eighteen-year-old Patrick Shortis (1893–1916) left his family in Ballybunion to follow a vocation to the priesthood. Less than five years later, wearing the green uniform of the Irish Volunteers, he followed Michael O'Rahilly in a fatal dash from the burning GPO to Moore Street. His niece and nephew, Mary and Richard Johnson, acknowledge his bravery but are pragmatic about their connection to the 1916 rebel and disinclined to invest in romantic eulogy. Richard observes: 'As you know, dead men tell no tales, and the vast majority of the mythology of 1916 was produced by live men and women telling tales.'

In the early 1900s Shortis won a 'first-class scholarship in his entrance exam to St Brendan's seminary in Killarney', where, his niece feels, he received both ecclesiastical instruction and 'an education in nationalism'. At eighteen, his vocational path led him to All Hallows College in Dublin, but after two years, and having gained a BA from the National University, he acknowledged that he found more inspiration in Marconi's experiments in wireless telegraphy than in theological debate.

In 1913 the young Kerryman returned to his native county to train as a wireless operator in the Atlantic Wireless College in Cahersiveen – the same institution at which Con Keating trained and from which he would later seek to steal radio equipment in the doomed operation that fell apart at Ballykissane – and left for London soon afterwards to sit his examinations for certification.

Patrick's prolonged absence from home meant that Ann Shortis, born in 1904, had very few memories of her eldest brother. 'She was very young when he left,' her daughter Mary says. 'She remembered saying goodbye to him [but] that was it.' Ann's young life had already been tainted by tragedy, having lost both her parents before she was two years old. Her mother, Annie, died in childbirth in 1905 and her father, William, died a few months later, leaving Ann and her six siblings in the care of 'two maternal aunts'. Norah and Mary Browne cared for the children and employed managers 'to look after their father's successful public house' on the main street in Ballybunion. But Ann's fair-haired eldest brother left almost immediately and she did not see him again.

Shortis passed his examinations in London but was denied his certificate, according to *Kerry's Fighting Story*, 'owing to his views on Irish affairs'. Like so many Irish emigrants in the early twentieth century, those views drew him into the orbit of the Irish nationalist movement in the city, and very possibly into the same Gaelic League halls frequented by fellow Kerrymen Michael Mulvihill, Patrick O'Connor and Denis Daly.

Shortis supported himself by working in Harrods department store in London's Knightsbridge but, according to his nephew, 'he came back [to Dublin] for the Rising about the same time as Michael Collins'. Shortly after his repatriation in January 1916, Shortis attended a meeting at 2 Dawson Street, where he was introduced to newly promoted deputy adjutant to the Dublin Brigade, Michael W. O'Reilly. In his BMH witness statement, O'Reilly said that the young Kerryman was one of 'a number of the Irish boys who had returned from England consequent upon the introduction of conscription there'. Shortis accepted O'Reilly's invitation to stay at this home in Fairview, and joined 'F' Company, 2nd Battalion, Dublin Brigade.

Captain Frank Henderson's small but close-knit Fairview Company drilled weekly in Fr Mathew Park. On the Thursday night before Holy Week, Commandant Thomas MacDonagh visited 'F' Company to deliver what twenty-year-old Volunteer Charles Saurin called a 'pep talk' in his BMH statement. MacDonagh told them that the 'manoeuvres which were taking place on Easter Sunday were most important' and 'if any man was not prepared to fight, now was his time to get out'. Volunteer Harry Colley recalled in his BMH statement: 'He did not tell us directly we were going out in rebellion but to me, at any rate, it was clear that the hour had come.'

Demobilised on Sunday after the confusion of MacNeill's countermand, 'F' Company received new mobilisation orders on Easter Monday. Saurin and Shortis arrived at Fr Mathew Park at 10.30 a.m. to discover that many of their number had reported directly to MacDonagh at Jacob's Biscuit Factory to the south of the city centre. While Captain Weafer, the senior officer present, awaited further orders, Saurin recounted how a young priest arrived to give general absolution and preach preparedness for the 'sacrifice we might have to make before long and the need to be prepared for it'.

Confusion reigned as conflicting orders arrived in Fairview, and shortly after midday Weafer instructed his men to 'go home and await further orders'. Advised not to go too far from the mobilisation point, Shortis invited Saurin, Seamus Daly and Henry Coyle to wait with him in O'Reilly's home in Foster Terrace. Saurin, who was already well equipped with his Martini Henry single-shot rifle, a .38 revolver and a large sheath knife, remembered that the young Kerryman 'provided us with food during our stay there and added to my armament by presenting me with a small automatic pistol and ammunition'.

In the late afternoon the small band was recalled to Fr Mathew Park, where they heard reports that the GPO had been taken and rumours of a cavalry charge down Sackville Street. Organised into three units, the 120 Volunteers of the 2nd Battalion moved out. Leo Henderson's advance guard engaged British troops approaching from Dollymount in the afternoon and Captain Frank Henderson's rearguard seized premises commanding Tolka Bridge. Captain Weafer led the remaining Volunteers into the city and was dispatched to an outpost at O'Connell Bridge.

By Tuesday the Henderson brothers had reached Volunteer Headquarters and James Connolly directed their men to reinforce the garrisons at the Imperial and Metropole hotels. It remains unclear where exactly Shortis was stationed for the two subsequent days but, on Friday, Cumann na mBan member Aoife de Burca found him at his post at the barricaded windows at the front of the besieged GPO. In her BMH statement, she recounted how 'Between 3 and 4 p.m. I got the smell of burning and knew that the GPO had taken fire. About this time the shelling was terrific, sometimes the whole place shook.' She remembered 'a Volunteer asking me would I say the Rosary with him at his post of duty; I did so, and got some other girls to join ... and every minute I thought a bomb or bullet would put an end to the lot of us'.

De Burca did not know who this Volunteer was at the time, but she testified that:

> Some months later, I think, I recognised the Volunteer of the Rosary ... from a photo in the *Catholic Bulletin*, and there, I'm sorry to say, I learned he was shot in the rush out from headqrs.; his name was given in the "C.B" as Shortis; poor fellow, the Rosary he asked me to say with him was probably his last, and fervently he said it.

Patrick Shortis volunteered to join Michael O'Rahilly's vanguard in the evacuation from the GPO on Friday evening and was fatally wounded in the first furious volley of machine-gun fire from the British barricade at the Parnell Street end of Moore Street. Volunteer Henry Coyle, with whom Shortis had shared his rations in Fairview on Easter Monday, fell beside him.

Richard Johnson is deeply frustrated by the dearth of information about his uncle's last days:

> There is nothing much to research. I mean his name is in the Roll of Honour in the National Museum in Kildare Street. I've been in there and seen that, but that's as far as any of us can go really. My mother talked to me but she didn't have much to say because none of the family knew where he was or what he was involved in. In fact, he had been dead for some considerable time before they heard about it; they never knew it.

According to family history, Patrick's brother, Archie, who was a student of chemistry in Dublin in 1916, developed TB 'as a result of being out at night looking for Uncle Paddy's body'. In a tale of grim coincidence, Richard says that it was actually his own father, also called Richard Johnson, who was the first person to find Paddy's body in the city morgue:

> My father was a student in Limerick in 1916 … but when he heard about the Rising he came up to Dublin to see what was happening … He saw the women in the street outside Jacob's factory cursing the Volunteers coming out. This, of course, was down near the Liberties in the city of Dublin where almost every single house would have had a member of the British armed forces among them. [He was not a member of the Volunteers] but had attended The O'Rahilly's Irish classes and knew the family, and Madam O'Rahilly asked Richard to look for her husband. He didn't find him, but in the morgue he came across a tall blond guy called Shortis. He came across [him] completely by accident, and then nearly twelve years later, he married my mother, the sister of the man he had seen lying out on a slab in the morgue.

When news finally reached Ballybunion that Shortis's body had been found, his siblings mourned his loss and carried the heavy burden of association with a rebel of 1916. His brothers Archie and Arnold both emigrated to the United States in the 1920s, ostensibly for 'health reasons' and 'to find work', but Richard feels that there may have been more to the story of his uncles' emigration: 'They were both on the run [during] the War of Independence.' The Black and Tans 'raided the house in Ballybunion a number of times and they were looking for them'. The brothers, like so many others, 'disappeared' in America.

'Uncle Bill', another of the Shortis brothers, 'didn't get involved in the War of Independence but got involved in the Civil War on the Irregular side'. He told his nephew that 'he was studying medicine in Galway University at the time', and he and his flying column 'occupied two very nice houses, Carton being one and the other being Lyons. He moved in very high quality circles,' Richard laughs. He was interned in the Curragh in 1922, 'but he never wanted to talk about it – too many unhappy memories and too many bitter memories'.

Ann Shortis's children, however, were served 'the Civil War for breakfast every day'.

Richard smiles at his parents' 'illogical' union, because 'they were totally antipathetic from the point of view of politics'. His father, Richard, the first district court justice to be appointed by the Free State, was a staunch Fine Gael supporter, while Ann, who 'had lost a number of brothers' to death and emigration, was 'republican more than anything else'. They had 'extremely heated arguments' about politics. It was 'volatile' but 'wonderful'.

Richard's parents didn't attend the ceremonies in Dublin during the Golden Jubilee but, in October 1966, Ann was proud to attend the unveiling of a memorial plaque dedicated to the memory of her brother on the house in Main Street, Ballybunion, where he was born in 1893.

THE AFTERMATH
OF THE RISING IN
THE KERRYMAN

REBELS NOT A HORDE

Saturday 13 May 1916

WELL ORGANISED AND HANDLED ARMY
(From the 'Daily Mail')

A man of long experience of Irish and Irish-American affairs who knows the whole of Ireland intimately and has just returned from Dublin, said yesterday: 'This is really a critical moment for the pursuance of a policy in Ireland which will put down the Sinn Fein movement for all time. If there is anything like wavering now in dealing with this rebellion on the score that it has merely been the error of a number of misguided people which ought to be looked over – that will be fate.

'The first and greatest mishap in connection with the movement was the discovery of the auxiliary ship off the west coast of Ireland disguised as a Dutch tramp steamer. She had on board, I believe, 25,000 stand [*sic*] of arms, machine guns, and ammunition. There is reason to infer that she had German military officers on board. If her crew had got this ship safely into the Shannon, for which she was making, the whole rebellion movement would have had a very different complexion.

'The way in which the ship went down was significant. The captain of the vessel which discovered the auxiliary told me that when those on board the latter found escape was hopeless, as they did at once, they hoisted the German flag, gave three cheers and sank their ship.

SKILLED PLAN IN DETAIL

'The plans for the rebellion give evidence of military efficiency and thoroughness. One who had seen a copy of the orders issued to the various rebel leaders in different places told me that the order for Dublin was given in the greatest detail and enumerated all the particular places to be seized. And as it turned out, possibly with one exception, the rebels did not make a mistake in carrying out the details of the order. They seized various strategic points in accordance with an extremely clever and comprehensive plan, matured and carried out with very great skill.

'Apart from the loss of the auxiliary ship all the points in the rebel's scheme worked out in their favour until Saturday. I cannot see that anything miscarried. The effect of a prolonged rebel success in Dublin or different parts of Ireland must not be overlooked. It is no reflection on the loyalty of Ireland as a whole to point out that others might have been led astray by a movement which worked on ignorance and passion, and which appeared to be succeeding. In one way and another, the situation would have meant a diversion which no doubt was what Germany intended!

'This was a thoroughly business-like rebellion. Everything in it shows organisation. What had been going on for a long time before the outbreak illustrated the efficiency and ability of the Sinn Feiners as a military body. They were as well armed as the British soldier. That was known. They had been drilling openly. They had a sham fight in Dublin some weeks ago, and even rehearsed the taking of the Castle gate. In their way they behaved as an army during the rising. They shot at every man who appeared in uniform and everyone who interfered on his behalf, but otherwise they did not shoot anyone. They were absolutely in hand – which shows organisation. As for the burning which took place it was a mishap as far as I could see.

'This was a real business, this rebellion. The plan miscarried.'

A PLEA FOR MERCY

Saturday 13 May 1916

'WIDE DISPARITY IN THE DEGREE OF GUILT'

The 'Irish Independent' says:– As we have previously said, we believe that justice should be tempered with mercy in dealing with the general body of the participants in the rising. As the 'Irish Times' said on Friday the prisoners who have been taken include many decent young fellows and hundreds of lads, some of whom are almost children. 'It is certain,' says our contemporary, 'that hundreds of the rebels were the dupes of cleverer men, some of whom, perhaps, were the dupes of their own fantastic imaginings.' As between the organisers and leaders of the revolt and many of their followers there is a wide disparity in the degree of guilt, and for this every possible allowance should be made. To the credit of the insurgents it must be said that they took no part in looting the city, but, on the contrary, made some efforts to prevent it. The public, as a whole, cannot be unmindful of the terrible consequences which have followed the outbreak, when they think of those to whom it owes its origin. But the sympathy which they may withhold from the leaders, they will extend to those who were victims rather than masters of the circumstances by which they were surrounded.

TRALEEMAN WOUNDED IN DUBLIN

Saturday 13 May 1916

Mr Christie O'Halloran, son of Mr Patrick O'Halloran, Staughton's Row, Tralee, was shot through the door while engaged as chemist's assistant in Montgomery's establishment in Dame St. We are so glad to learn that the wound is not serious.

EXPLOSIVES IN THE G.P.O.

Saturday 13 May 1916

On Sunday the military guarding Sackville Street warned the few people who were let pass through the street that they ought not to remain near the General Post Office, as there was danger of an explosion of dynamite, which the insurgents had brought into the building. The explosion did not occur; but that day a number of bombs were found in the ruins. They were made of salmon tins with fuses attached, and had they gone off might have done much damage. Since Sunday the work of searching the ruins has gone on and many strange things have been brought to light. Yesterday morning, a box holding gelignite was found. Handed over to Police Inspector Barrett, it was brought by his order to a safe place until it could be examined by military officers.

'KATIE, I'M DONE!'

Saturday 13 May 1916

GIRL SHOT DEAD IN A ROOM DURING THE RISING
HER COMPANION'S PATHETIC STORY

The intelligence has been received that a Miss Janie Costello, shorthand writer and typist, was shot dead in Dublin on 27th April, and was buried in Glasnevin on 1st May.

She was a native of Glenfield, Kilmallock. The sad news of her tragic death has evoked feelings of the deepest regret, and the utmost sympathy will go forth to the parents in their great sorrow.

A girl friend (Miss Katie Lewis) writes to her parents:–

'I, for one, will never forget the Irish rebellion. One of the chief firing lines was outside our windows. Now prepare yourselves for the greatest shock you ever got in your life. Janie Costello is sleeping her last sleep in Glasnevin since the 1st May. My poor child was shot dead before my eyes in our bedroom. The firing had ceased.

'Unfortunately, she raised the window, turned away instantly and was shot through both lungs. I heard no sound as she stopped the bullet herself. All she said was, "I'm shot, oh Katie, I'm done", and fell lifeless. I knew she was gone.

'Before he had time to reload, I was through the door for assistance which I had gotten in a few seconds. One bullet lodged in the jamb of the door, about one and a half inches above Mrs Hanlon's head, I discovered one bullet.

'I searched everywhere until I found the one in the door. It was a soldier's bullet.

'She was shot on the 27th April.

'Mr Bell kept on to the military for a permit to go on with the funeral arrangements and a pass to Glasnevin. That is all we wanted from them. Of course, the military would bury her, but, thank God, their assistance was not required.

'The best oak coffin in Dublin was got for her; also a lovely spot in Glasnevin, not far from the Parnell grave. They were allowing no friends to the cemetery, only the driver of the hearse, in some cases one friend to see the body interred.

'However five people saw Janie to the grave. As we were leaving Glasnevin, four hearses arrived with no one accompanying them but the drivers.

'Under the circumstances, more could not be done for Janie if she had thousands at her back. God help her, it was her fate; she was to go and I know she is better off.

'I knew she felt no pain, her face was as peaceful as though she were asleep. I seemed turned to stone since I left her behind me in Glasnevin but I am certain of one thing – she is in Heaven. She was at Holy Communion a few days before she died. She was after making a novena and she died a martyr's death.

'I folded her hands and closed her eyes, and who could touch her with more love, once? There are 60 unidentified bodies in the morgue. Hundreds of girls shot and Dublin in ruins. From Nelson's Pillar to O'Connell's Bridge is gone completely. I must now write to her mother.'

THE COUNTESS IN GREEN

Saturday 27 May 1916

SURRENDER KISS TO HER REVOLVER
(From the 'Daily Mail')

How Countess Markievitz [*sic*] surrendered with a force of 120 rebels who had been in possession of the Royal College of Surgeons all through the rebellion was related to a special correspondent of the 'Daily Mail', by a Dublin public official who crossed to England.

'Countess Markievitz was in command of the party which seized the college,' he said, 'and she defended it very stubbornly. It was the last place in St Stephen's Green to surrender. At eight o'clock on Saturday morning the white flag was hoisted in place of the rebel flag and a communication was sent to the officer commanding the attacking force to say that the garrison would surrender at eleven o'clock.

'At the appointed hour, the Countess marched out of the college, followed by her force walking in twos. She was dressed, as she had been throughout the week, entirely in green – green tunic, a green hat with a green feather in it, green puttees, and green boots. It was a rather picturesque scene. She led her men to the British force, saluted the officer in command, kissed her revolver before surrendering it and her bandolier to him, and then announced, "I am ready."' Her men were disarmed and marched under an armed escort through Grafton Street and Dame Street to the Castle.

'NIGHTMARE DAYS AND SLEEPLESS NIGHTS'

Saturday 24 June 1916

THE HON. ALBINIA BRODRICK'S EXPERIENCE DURING THE DUBLIN RISING

(Special to the 'Liberator' and 'Kerryman')

By Albinia Broderick

Those of us who have given both our hearts and our work to the country that we love, will not, while life lasts, forget the agony of those early days in the rising of 1916. To us, the glorious Easter moon must always bring to mind the prayers and the tears that mingled with them, when things seemed very dark, and life was suddenly overshadowed with tragedy. Some of those days I spent in England. After much time watching the station, we ascertained in Cork that the Rosslare train and boat would run for the first time again on Saturday, the 29th of April. There was nothing to be done in Ireland that could help anyone, and there was just a bare possibility that something, no matter how little, might be feasible in England. When history is a-making, even a little thing counts. My object was to lay before the authorities facts. For it has always been my experience during a varied life that the higher in power a man is, the less opportunity he has of knowing the real state of affairs. He is, in short, dependent on the reports of others. I also hoped to get some of the facts before the English public, through the Press. It was the easier for me to do this because I have never been a member of any physical force party, and I felt the rising to be a disaster, whilst I understood and deeply sympathised with the causes leading up to it. I also realized the great possibilities opened up, and

THE FINE OPPORTUNITY WHICH LAY READY TO THE HAND OF THE GOVERNMENT, IF THEY COULD EMBRACE IT.

It was a strange fortnight, full of interviews with authorities, with editors, with Members of Parliament, letters, telephone calls, press work. To my first object, another was immediately added. It was quickly brought home to me that the wives and mothers of Volunteers and others, in prison and deported, had no knowledge in many cases what had happened to their husbands and sons. They might be dead, wounded or prisoners. No lists were issued, and these innocent women were left in that agony of anxiety of which only a woman knows the meaning, for many days.

The Prime Minister, whom I saw in his private room in the House of Commons, listened with attention and interest to my short statement of the causes which produced the rising and of the new forces of progress and reform at present at work in Ireland. Looking back upon the interview I sometimes wonder how he came to listen so quietly to the home truths as I ticked them off from my list of notes. The holding up of the Home Rule Bill, the Castle Jobs, the appointment of Sir Matthew Nathan, the last appointments to a judgeship, the condoning of the Orange arming and gun-running, the deportations of Volunteers during the past year, previous to the rising of course, the taking away of the £2,000 grant for Irish and for Technical Education, the mean and objectionable attitude of the Department of Agriculture towards co-operation. Well, we know them all. I outlined

THE GROWING FEELING THAT THE PARLIAMENTARY PARTY NO LONGER REPRESENTED NATIONALIST IRELAND

and that a strong party had arisen which at present had no means of voicing its principles and its policy. I gave the New Forces, all extra-parliamentary: Co-operation, the Gaelic League, Sinn Fein and the Irish Volunteers – and noted to him that none of these could be dealt with through Mr Redmond, who was in sympathy with none of them. The Premier then asked what I would suggest; and partly then and partly in a subsequent letter, I ventured the following: suspension of the Lord Lieutenancy with a view to final abolition of Castle Rule in the near future, resignation of Sir Matthew Nathan (Mr. Birrell's resignation had been made public the same day), resignation of Mr. T. W. Russell and appointment of Sir Horace Plunkett in his place. Appointment of Lord MacDonnell as Chief Secretary, the finding of some direct means of communication with the party of reform, preferably through Eoin MacNeill – and, I think it was my final word, the avoidance of a past mistake – the making of martyrs. I was not there to ask for any mercy for anyone – no one, I think, sank to that level, throughout. My endeavour was as a mere looker-on, however deeply interested, to state facts as I saw them from a non-political standpoint. On Home Rule I did not venture to touch – added to which it was too obvious a remedy to need suggestion. I asked for leave to go round the prisons, to get the names and addresses of the men deported, for the sake of their womenfolk – but found that that was a matter for the military. Curiously enough, when I visited the war office and saw Lord Kitchener's private secretary (who went down with him in the 'Hampshire'), I found it was not in their department either! My letter to the Press on the subject appeared in the *Westminster Review*, and just at the same time a rather belated question was asked in Parliament. Lists were issued later.

Some of my interviews had their amusing side,

ONE CABINET MINISTER, WHO OUGHT TO HAVE KNOWN BETTER, HAD NEVER HEARD OF EOIN MACNEILL.

One of the most prominent Ulstermen gravely spoke of the horrible guilt of the rebels, and in the next breath assured me that what they had done in Ulster was deliberate and they would do it again, if necessary. A leading newspaper proprietor, pointing to the tattered remains of the Carlow mail-bag and to a home-made bayonet taken in Dublin, considered those a sufficient reply to my statements.

Throughout that fortnight, one was filled with amazement at the possibility of so colossal an ignorance of things Irish, existing in England and in ordinary society. Where to begin, in talking of the rising, which, naturally enough was the chief, often the only subject of conversation, I did not know. Of history they knew nothing. Of our people they knew nothing; of the country they knew nothing. I gathered that

ENGLAND'S ONE ENDEAVOUR HAS BEEN TO CONTROL WITH FATHERLY KINDNESS A SET OF UNGRATEFUL SAVAGES.

One man was astonished when I assured him that I lived amongst those same 'savages' and loved them. Another, a lady, Anglo-Irish, leaning confidentially across the tea-table said to me: 'I am Irish, you know, and of course I would not say it to anyone but you – but you and I must admit to each other that the Irish people are slow, vulgar brutes.' 'Well,' I answered smoothly, 'where do you come from?' 'Oh, County –' 'Ah,' I said, 'no doubt the people of your county are just what you describe but let me tell you that my Kerry people are gentlemen.' Alas, she failed to catch my meaning. Irish Volunteers, Sinn Feiners, Citizen Army, were all boiled down comfortably into one body, the pronunciation of whose name was difficult, but distinctly connected with Original Sin, and a very nice, descriptive name too. It was both puzzling and shocking to them that, whereas I ought to have been ashamed and apologetic and generally humble, they found themselves unaccountably tangled up with information and reasoning unanswerable from out of their ignorance, all going to prove that

IRELAND, FROM A HIGHER SPHERE, LOOKED DOWN WITH SURPRISE ON ENGLAND AND THE ENGLISH.

It was not I who suggested that discussions on Ireland must cease. In justice I must chronicle the saying of one lady: 'I know nothing at all about this Irish business,' said she, 'but I can't help having sympathy with the rebels, because I always think they wouldn't have rebelled if they hadn't had something to rebel for.'

On the other hand, the knowledge of Ireland and the sympathy with her, shown by many Liberals, came as something of surprise to me also. When Sir Edward Carson in his speech in the House, spoke of 'recent events in Dublin which I so greatly regret' a voice cried: 'And well you may.' Such a shout arose thereon from the Government side of the House that he faltered, stopped, and was unable to take up the thread of his speech again.

We, in Ireland, owe a debt to such as these and to those writers and editors of the Liberal Press, who so finely championed an unpopular cause and told the English public truths which it was fitting they should know.

Those were nightmare days and sleepless nights. News from Ireland, except of executions, sentences of penal servitude and deportations was sadly to seek [*sic*]. 'Cork and Kerry normal' – these were the words one watched for eagerly in the morning's paper. Then came one dreadful day when 'Outbreak in Killarney' stared one in the face. That brought me home, and the quicker that I learned accidentally in Dublin that two thousand soldiers had left for Kerry on the previous day.

The evening before I shook the mud of London from my feet, I visited the Gaelic League offices where the raid on the papers had not yet been carried out. The day I left, a dear old friend of mine, a Kerry priest, asked me to lunch at one of the big restaurants, where our conversation, carried on in Irish, caused great surprise. It took the other guests a little while to decide whether we were a pair of lunatics or Belgian refugees. Unfortunately, we never ascertained their decision.

ASSAULTING A POLICE CONSTABLE

Saturday 24 June 1916

CHARGE AGAINST A KILLORGLIN MAN

At Killorglin Petty Sessions, before Messrs E. M. P. Wynne, R.M., R. Power and J. T. O'Connor.

District Inspector Cheesman, R.I.C. prosecuted John Clifford, of Langford Street, Killorglin, for disorderly conduct in Killorglin on the 1st of June whilst being drunk. On a second summons, he was charged with assaulting Constable Lucy, Killorglin.

Mr M. McCatie, solr., Killarney who defended Constable Lucy said on the 1st of June, about 11 p.m., there was a crowd at the corner of Langford Street and some shouting from the crowd. They went over to get them away and, when going towards them, John Clifford, the defendant, shouted: 'Up Sinn Féin.' He then walked away, and when going from the crowd, shouted again: 'We are Sinn Féiners until death.' He then ran away, and witness followed and caught him and arrested him on the charge of disorderly behaviour on the public street while being drunk.

The remainder of the crowd then ran up and when he saw the crowd coming, he struck witness with his clenched fist on the left ear, and made a second blow at him which he warded off. Sergeant McCaffery then came up and they brought him to the barrack. He lay down on the street and they had to drag him. The crowd followed and Clifford shouted: 'You are no good that you cannot save me', or words to that effect. The crowd followed to the barrack and a stone struck an inner door in the barrack. He saw a stone taken from Clifford's pocket by one of the police. He was drunk.

Sergeant McCaffery corroborated.

Chairman – We will convict in the case of the assault on Constable Lucy.

District Inspector – I will withdraw the summons for being drunk and disorderly.

Sergeant McCaffery, in reply to the bench said there were several previous convictions against him.

Chairman – Fined 21s and bound to the peace, himself in £10 and two sureties in £5 each for 12 months, in default, one month in gaol.

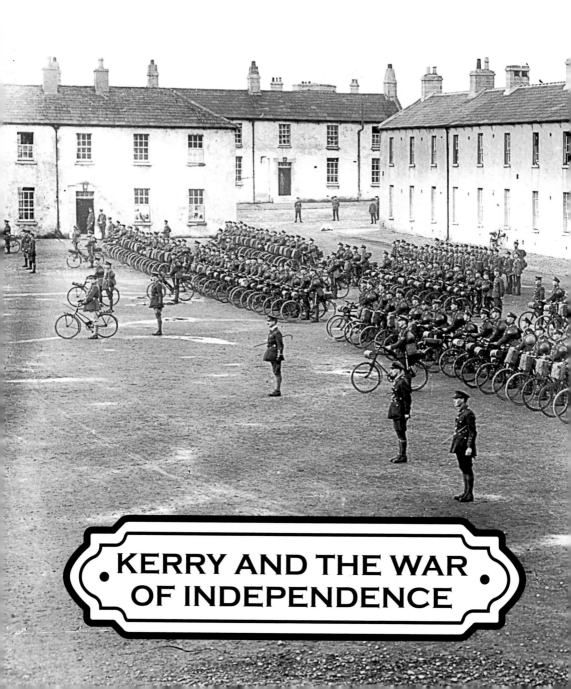

KERRY AND THE WAR OF INDEPENDENCE

'PRACTICALLY ALL THE RIC' ONSIDE IN KERRY

Ryle Dwyer

YEARS later, when people looked back on the War of Independence and the Civil War, their views were often coloured by the 1916 fiascos in Kerry. In a biography of Richard Mulcahy, the chief of staff of the IRA, his son Risteard wrote that his father could never understand why the Civil War was so bitter in Kerry when they did so little during the War of Independence. 'Kerry's entire record in the Black and Tan struggle consisted in shooting an unfortunate soldier the day of the Truce,' General Eoin O'Duffy, who served for a time as Mulcahy's deputy chief of staff, told a gathering in Bandon, County Cork, on 15 October 1933.

There is no doubt that those views were grossly distorted. Indeed, over the years many misconceptions have developed about the independence struggle. It was not – as has often been supposed – the executions following the Easter Rising that drove the Irish people firmly into the arms of Sinn Féin, so much as the introduction of the bill to establish compulsory military service in Ireland in April 1918, an act which provoked a sense of outrage throughout the island.

On 10 April 1918, as the anger was at its height, seven members of the Bally-macelligott Company of the Irish Volunteers – John Cronin, Maurice Carmody, Maurice Reidy, John Browne, Richard Laide, John Flynn and the captain of the company, Tom McEllistrim – decided to arm themselves properly to resist conscription by raiding the RIC barracks at Gortatlea for weapons. They planned the raid for Saturday night, 13 April, while two of the four RIC men stationed there would be out on routine patrol.

After Sergeant Martin Boyle and Constable Patrick Fallon had gone on patrol, McEllistrim and his colleagues began the raid on the barracks as the Cork to Tralee train was pulling into the railway station. However, Boyle and Fallon, who were both armed, saw them from the railway station. They slipped up to the open door of the barracks, where they could see what was going on inside.

The two RIC men claimed that the first shots were from inside the building, and that they had merely returned fire by shooting without aim into the crowded kitchen. But McEllistrim insisted that the two RIC men began shooting and that he and the others were caught completely by surprise. 'Browne was shot through the temple and the bullet came right out at the back of his head,' McEllistrim later said. Laide was also wounded and his colleagues brought him to a nearby house, but he died a few days later in hospital.

When people came to take Browne's body away, Constable Fallon, who was from Strabane, County Tyrone, was very dismissive. 'You can wrap the green flag round him,' he is reputed to have remarked.

Boyle and Fallon were transferred out of Kerry, but McEllistrim learned that they would be in Tralee on 14 June 1918 to give evidence in court. He and Cronin went to Tralee with plans to shoot the two RIC men. They brought two shotguns with them, hidden in a sack while they waited in a bar in The Mall. The street outside was very busy. As the policemen were heading from the court to the RIC barracks for their lunch, McEllistrim and Cronin assembled their guns and raced across the street.

'We lifted our guns to fire. We were now only ten yards from them,' McEllistrim later recalled. 'As we did they flung themselves backwards in a somewhat sitting position on the flags. We took aim and fired.' Fallon was hit in the back around the shoulder, which wasn't a fatal wound, while Boyle was missed altogether. In the ensuing panic, McEllistrim and Cronin dropped their shotguns in the middle of the street and fled the scene.

SENSATIONAL SHOOTING IN TRALEE

Saturday 22 June 1918

POLICEMEN FIRED AT

ONE SHOT THROUGH BACK

(From the 'Cork Examiner')

One of the most daring outrages in the whole history of the trouble in Ireland occurred in Tralee on Friday evening [14 June] when two policemen were shot at in the public street, entering the Square, shortly after two o'clock, by two young men, each armed with a shotgun. A young man named Sugrue was under trial before Mr Wynne, R.M., charged with perjury in his evidence at the Coroners Inquest into the deaths of two young men, Browne and Laide, who were fatally shot last April, during a raid for arms at Gortatlea Police Hut. The jury found that both deceased were shot by Constable Fallon and Sergeant Boyle.

At the adjournment of the perjury case Constable Fallon and Sergeant Boyle were on their way through the Mall to the Police barracks, when entering the Square two young men, each holding a gun, appeared in the street, took deliberate aim at the Constable and Sergeant, and fired, the shots going off simultaneously. Both men threw the guns on the street and disappeared. Fallon was shot through the back, near the shoulder, and was removed to the Infirmary.

A scene of the wildest excitement followed. The police rushed pell mell to the Barracks, and crowds congregated in the streets in excited groups inquiring into and discussing the sensational occurrence. Police under arms are scouring the town and district for the perpetrators of the deed.

TWO ARRESTS

Saturday 22 June 1918

SERGEANT FALLON'S CONDITION

Two men, named Browne, Feale's Bridge and Carmody, Clogher, were arrested during the night in connection with the shooting occurrence in Tralee on Friday.

Three marks left by the shots on Mr. Frank McDonnell's house next to The Square, attract attention.

Considering the great number of people in the Mall at the time of the shooting, it is miraculous there was no civilian shot.

On inquiring at the county infirmary to-day (Saturday), we were told Sergt. Fallon's condition is not serious as the 'pellets', which were of a specially large type, only wounded his shoulder.

Tralee's main street as it looked at the start of the twentieth century.

During the remainder of 1918 and into 1919 tensions gradually increased in Kerry and 1920 saw the shooting of a number of RIC men and arms raids on RIC barracks around the county. The British responded by introducing the Black and Tans as auxiliary policemen to bolster the RIC. The Tans were essentially foreigners confronting native rebels, and as they harassed local people they inevitably drove the population more solidly behind the rebels. Being outsiders, they were also heavily dependent on the RIC for local knowledge.

Little over a fortnight after his appointment as RIC divisional commissioner for Munster, Lieutenant Colonel Gerald Bryce Ferguson Smyth visited Listowel on 19 June 1920. 'Sinn Féin has had all the sport up to the present, and we are going to have sport now,' Smyth told the local RIC. 'We must take the offensive and beat Sinn Féin at its own tactics.' He elaborated:

When civilians approach shout, 'Hands Up!' Should the order not be immediately obeyed, shoot, and shoot with effect. If persons approaching carry their hands in their pockets, or are suspicious-looking, shoot them down. You may make mistakes occasionally, and innocent persons may be shot, but that cannot be helped. No policeman will get into trouble for shooting any man.

One of the constables, Jeremiah Mee, replied indignantly, 'By your accent I take it you are an Englishman, and in your ignorance you forget you are addressing Irishmen.' He took off his cap and belt and threw them onto a table. 'These too, are English,' he said. 'Take them as a present from me, and to hell with you, you murderer.'

Mee and four other constables – Michael Fitzgerald, John O'Donovan, Patrick Sheeran and Thomas Hughes – promptly quit the RIC in what became known as 'the Listowel Mutiny'. Hughes later joined the priesthood and became a Catholic bishop in Nigeria, while Mee offered his services to Sinn Féin and the IRA. Michael Collins utilised Mee for propaganda purposes.

The Listowel mutiny was symptomatic of what was happening within the RIC. As the conflict got dirtier, members of the RIC were confronted with the stark choice of supporting the Tans, or their fellow countrymen. Many chose to supply information to the IRA, which probably explains why comparatively few RIC men were killed in Kerry. Tadhg Kennedy, the intelligence officer for the Kerry No. 1 Brigade, had little difficulty in securing information from the local RIC men. 'Practically all the RIC with few exceptions were on our side,' he testified in his BMH statement.

He received invaluable assistance from people like RIC County Inspector James Duffy and his successor William Beanney, along with Crimes Special Sergeant Thomas O'Rourke and his successor Sergeant William Costello, as well as

The RIC lead the Corpus Christi procession along New Street in Killarney, 1913.
(Courtesy of the MacMonagle Collection)

District Inspector Bernard O'Connor in Dingle. Sergeant Clarke in Tralee was not prepared to co-operate, but Clarke's wife was passing on valuable information to Kennedy to protect her husband for the sake of their family. Maybe they would have taken him out if she had not been so helpful.

In the circumstances it was hardly surprising that only a select few senior officers were targeted in Kerry. RIC District Inspector Tobias O'Sullivan was shot in Listowel on 20 January 1921. Major John A. MacKinnon, the head of 'H' Company of the Auxiliaries, was killed in Tralee on 15 April 1921. Head Constable William K. Storey was killed in Castleisland on 8 May 1921, and Head Constable Francis Benson was shot dead in Tralee six days later.

The biggest attack on the British Army in Ireland during the War of Independence was in Kerry, at Headford Junction (almost seven miles from Killarney). It took place on 21 March 1921, when thirty-two Volunteers took on a force of between thirty and fifty British soldiers. Strangely, Dorothy Macardle did not mention the battle in her mammoth book *The Irish Republic*, and Charles

Commandant Dan Allman of the IRA's East Kerry Brigade, who was killed at Headford Cross on 21 March 1921. (Courtesy of Mercier Press)

Townshend also overlooked it in his *The British Campaign in Ireland 1919–1921*. The Kerry No. 2 Brigade of the IRA ambushed a train carrying one officer and twenty-nine other ranks of the 1st Royal Fusiliers. The troops detrained and the ensuing gunfight lasted for some fifty minutes, until the arrival of another train with more soldiers forced the attackers to withdraw.

The Irish Times described the battle as 'one of the fiercest that has yet taken place between crown forces and rebels in the South of Ireland'. Officially, one British officer, Lieutenant C. F. Adams, and six other ranks were killed, and twelve were wounded, two of whom subsequently died of their wounds. On the IRA side, Dan Allman, one of the co-leaders of the attack died at the scene, along with Jimmy Bailey. Three civilian passengers, all cattle dealers, also died. John Breen of Killarney was killed on the spot, while Patrick O'Donoghue of Killarney and Michael Cagney of Ballyfane, Liscarroll, were mortally wounded.

TOM McELLISTRIM

Simon Brouder

TOM McEllistrim (1894–1973), who served as a TD for North Kerry for five decades, was a key figure in the county during both the War of Independence and the Civil War. McEllistrim joined the Ballymacelligott Company of the Irish Volunteers in 1914 and was one of the men recruited to unload the German guns from the *Aud* if they had made it to Fenit. After the Rising he was interned by the British in Frongoch Internment Camp.

In one of his most significant acts in the post-Rising period he led an arms raid on Gortatlea RIC Barracks in April 1918, which was one of the first incidents of guerrilla warfare in the period. In fact, the Gortatlea attack is often cited as the first true act of the War of Independence, which did not officially begin until the following January.

McEllistrim served in the IRA in Kerry throughout the War of Independence and he was instrumental in the setting up of a full-time guerrilla unit in the IRA's Kerry No. 2 Brigade. His column fought in both the Clonbanin Ambush, which took place in Cork on 5 March 1921 – where 100 Volunteers took on a British Army convoy carrying forty soldiers and Brigadier General Hanway Robert Cumming – and in the famous Headford Ambush on 21 March 1921. At the latter action, the IRA ambushed a train carrying British troops and Dan Allman, the leader of the guerrilla unit, was killed. This left McEllistrim in command.

McEllistrim arguably played as important a role in the War of Independence as Tom Barry or Dan Breen. As noted above, he was involved in the Gortatlea arms raid in 1918, was a core founder and later leader of one of the largest and most active flying columns in the south-west region, and took part in the Clonbanin Ambush, where Brigadier General H. R. Cumming was killed – the highest ranking

British officer killed during the War of Independence. However, as McEllistrim did not write a book about his exploits and was not prepared to talk about them publicly, he has not attained the same historical fame as Barry or Breen.

McEllistrim rejected the Anglo-Irish Treaty and was one of the senior IRA figures in Kerry during the Civil War. In the war's early months he commanded a flying column in the fighting in Limerick city, before returning to Kerry.

McEllistrim was elected to the Dáil in 1923 and he remained a TD until 1969. His son and grandson, both also named Tom, followed him into Fianna Fáil and the Dáil.

The IRA garrison at Farranfore Barracks in 1922. Included in the picture are Tom McEllistrim, Johnny O'Connor, Mossie Galvin and Tommy Woods.
(Courtesy of Mercier Press)

CAMP BARRACKS ATTACKED

Saturday 21 February 1920

WALL BLOWN AWAY

FIERCE BATTLE

POLICE SERGEANT WOUNDED

Wires Cut – Roads Turned Up

An armed attack on the Camp Police Barracks commenced at about one o'clock on Thursday morning.

The attackers used hand grenades, rifles, revolvers and crowbars.

Sergeant McDonagh and six men stationed in the barracks replied with rifle fire and hand grenades.

After a battle lasting over an hour the raiders succeeded in blowing up the end wall of the barracks and called for surrender of the police.

The latter, however, refused and kept up a brisk fire on the attackers who ultimately withdrew, leaving behind them two guns, a colter revolver [*sic*] and a couple of crow bars.

Sergeant McDonagh was shot through the cheek, and so far as can be ascertained, this was the only casualty.

The telegraph and telephone wires were cut in a wide area at both sides of Tralee district, and the roads were blocked with trees and other barricades.

The road from Tralee to Camp was cut across near Anna, and the military motor lorries were unable to proceed.

The road leading from Tralee to Ardfert was blocked with fallen trees and the telegraph wires were tangled across the road. …

When the Blennerville road was made passable Sergeant McDonagh was removed to Tralee Military hospital, where it was found that the wound in his face is not of a serious nature.

CIVILIAN SHOT BY POLICEMAN

Saturday 21 February 1920

At 8.30 on Friday night a highly sensational incident occurred in the village of Ballylongford, an ancient but ever peaceful centre in North Kerry, about eight miles from Listowel. About the hour mentioned a respectable young man of about 19 years of age, named John Heaphey, was leaving the village for his home at Carrig, and when at the west side of the 'Old Bridge' was shot at from behind, and on turning round saw a police constable after firing. Previous to the occurrence the same constable was seen to fire three or four shots, the last one of which lodged in the right lung of young Heaphey, who has since been conveyed to St. John's Hospital, Limerick, in a precarious condition. On inquiries being made by our Listowel correspondent he learned that the ex-English soldier R.I.C. man has not been placed under arrest and that it was not probable that he would [be].

CAHERDANIEL TRAGEDY

Saturday 20 March 1920

COURTHOUSE CARETAKER SHOT DEAD

Cornelius Kelly, sailor, aged 40, was shot dead by six armed men in Caherdaniel, south Kerry, between 9 and 10 o'clock on Tuesday night.

Deceased was a caretaker of Caherdaniel Courthouse, where three bicycles belonging to the police were stored a couple of days previously. After Kelly was shot dead the raiders carried off the bicycles.

PADDY FOLEY'S BRUTAL END

Ryle Dwyer

RIC Constable Paddy Foley from the Annascaul area was targeted early in Kerry. One of a large family, he was reared by a childless aunt and uncle with a view to inheriting their farm. Following the outbreak of the First World War he ran away to join the Royal Munster Fusiliers. Although under age, he made it to the Front and was captured by the Germans. He then spent four years as a prisoner of war.

In January 1920 he joined the RIC and was stationed in Galway. One day he turned up at his first cousin Tadhg Kennedy's digs in Nelson Street, Tralee. While he was staying with Kennedy in Tralee, Na Fianna reported seeing him enter the RIC barracks on a number of occasions. 'I advised him not to go back home,' Kennedy noted.

Foley insisted on returning to Annascaul, however, so Kennedy decided to keep an eye on him. They travelled to Annascaul together by train and had a meal at Kennedy's home. 'I again tried to persuade him to clear out,' Kennedy recalled, 'but he wouldn't take any notice of my advice.'

Some days later the RIC district inspector in Dingle, Bernard O'Connor, who had been supplying Kennedy with information, handed over notebooks that Foley had given him at the RIC station in Dingle. They provided 'the names of every IRA officer in the district and every prominent Sinn Féiner', including many of Foley's own cousins, according to Kennedy. He passed those on to Brigade Commandant Paddy Cahill, who was also a cousin of Foley. 'It was a very painful situation for Cahill and myself,' according to Kennedy.

Foley was seized coming out of Moriarty's Hotel in Annascaul on 21 April 1920. Fr Edmond Walsh, a Franciscan priest, gave him the last rites and the local IRA then executed him. His bullet-ridden body was found at Deelis near Castlegregory, about seven miles from his home, two days later. He had been shot multiple times, with a blindfold around his eyes and his hands tied behind his back.

The gruesome killing made the front pages internationally in newspapers such as the *New York Tribune, New York Evening World, Washington Herald* and even the *El Paso Herald* in Texas and the *Ogden Standard-Examiner* in Utah.

BODY SHATTERED WITH BULLETS AT DEELIS

Saturday 24 April 1920

GRUESOME DETAILS OF THE OCCURRENCE
VICTIM BLINDFOLDED AND SODDEN WITH BLOOD

In the auxiliary creamery yard at Deelis, Castlegregory of Mr J. M. Slattery and Sons, on Friday morning at 7 o'clock, was found the body of Patrick Foley of Aunascaul [*sic*], an ex-soldier and a member of the R.I.C. since January last, with his hands tied tightly behind his back and his eyes blindfolded, by a handkerchief, which was tied about his head, and twenty-six bullet holes in his body, nearly all within the region of the chest.

The body was lying in the centre of a large yard, in front of the creamery, on its back, and the position would suggest that it remained as it fell after being shot.

Underneath the head and shoulders was a pool of blood which flowed freely down the hollow of the yard when the body was disturbed on examination by the police and military.

SINN FÉIN COURTS IN DINGLE

Saturday 15 May 1920

MIDNIGHT PROCEEDINGS
DAYLIGHT ARRESTS
WORKHOUSE AS A PRISON
Money and Goods Recovered

Great excitement was created on Saturday last when three arrests were made early one evening by the Dingle Volunteers. The effect on the three persons arrested, and indeed, on the general public was rather startling. The prisoners were placed under guard in the Carnegie Library and detained until late at night, when they were tried before a jury of Sinn Féin and Volunteer officers. Only Volunteers and about eight witnesses were allowed into the hall during the proceedings, which continued until about 12.30 a.m. The arrests were made in connection with the taking recently of pipes, tobacco and sweets to the value of £10, from the premises of Mr Michael O'Halloran, Green Street. The secret service of the Sinn Féiners seems to have been very reliable. The prisoners were proved guilty, and a good deal of the missing property was recovered. During the proceedings, the street in front of Carnegie Hall was thronged with people. The crowd included half a dozen dumb-founded policemen.

The above proceedings did not, however, complete the Sinn Fein activities of the night. Whilst the crowd pressed round the Carnegie Hall from 10 p.m. till 12.30, four other arrests were quietly made by another section of Sinn Fein police in different houses in the town and country. The prisoners are said to have been conveyed to and detained in a disused wing of the workhouse, where the court again assembled at 3 a.m. in this case on Monday morning, and tried them. The charge against the prisoners was that they had broken into and taken away a considerable sum of Old Age Pensions money from the Ventry Post Office. Sinn Fein and Volunteers officers here maintain very great reticence in regard to the proceedings of the court, and the only information available is that after preliminary denials the four concerned pleaded guilty and promised to hand over the money. They were detained under guard until late on Tuesday night when all the money was handed over to the court. This has been verified on today (Thursday) by our correspondent, who has been informed that all the Old Age Pension money taken from Ventry Post Office on 22nd was yesterday actually handed in to the Sub-Postmistress there by a prominent Sinn Feiner, with the notification that it had been recovered by the Sinn Fein Court.

Most of the identical 10s. notes taken from the Post Office a fortnight ago have been recovered we are told.

Very great satisfaction is felt locally at this latest phase of Sinn Fein activities. For a long time there has been no security for the property of the citizens, and evil disposed persons were inclined to think that they had a free hand.

SINN FÉIN COURT AT ARDFERT

Saturday 29 May 1920

The four young men, who were arrested in the village of Ardfert on Thursday night last by Volunteers and conveyed to some unknown destination, were tried by a Volunteer Courtmartial, constituted of four officers, on Sunday evening last, on charges of the larceny of bicycles and two of being accomplices in the crime.

PRECAUTIONS IN COURT

The court was guarded by a section of Volunteers standing to attention and bearing rifles and bayonets, and the prisoners were kept blindfolded while the proceedings were in progress.

FACILITIES FOR DEFENCE

The prisoners were accorded every facility to defend themselves. A Volunteer officer was chosen as their advocate, and statements were taken from every person they nominated to be able to give evidence to refute the charges. ...

Eventually two, against whom there was a great weight of evidence, pleaded guilty, and appealed to the court to be treated leniently. They promised they would not be guilty of any such offence again, and would abide by the law in future, and revealed the hiding places in which the two bicycles were kept. As well, for any damages which the machines had suffered, they agreed to make good.

WILL NOT COMMIT THEMSELVES AGAIN

The two remaining prisoners pleaded guilty to minor offences, and were left out under the First Offenders' Act. They too gave their words to be law-abiding citizens and were warned by the court that they would be dealt with severely if they committed themselves again.

TADHG KENNEDY AND THE INTELLIGENCE WAR

Simon Brouder

THOUGH less well known than the likes of Austin Stack, one Kerryman in particular, Tadhg 'Tim' Kennedy (1885–1955) from Annascaul, played a pivotal role in the War of Independence, both in Kerry and nationally. In 1905 he moved to Tralee from West Kerry and took up a role with Kerry County Council. An enthusiast of the national cause and all things Gaelic, he soon became secretary of the Tralee Gaelic League Branch and also a member of the GAA County Board. His nationalist leanings saw him become friends with Austin Stack, who swore him in to the local IRB. Kennedy met Michael Collins in 1913 and the pair also became fast friends. Late that same year Kennedy was contacted by a member of the Volunteer executive in Dublin and asked to form a corps in Tralee, which he did using the local Gaelic League branch as its nucleus.

His first major involvement in militant nationalism came in 1916, when he was appointed by Stack to lead the Dingle Volunteers during the planned Easter Rising. Kennedy and his West Kerry Volunteer troops made it as far as Tralee, only to find out the planned national rebellion had been called off.

Throughout the War of Independence Kennedy mimicked Collins's tactics in Dublin. He formed a sophisticated network in Kerry that was closely modelled on Collins's intelligence apparatus in Dublin. Collins and Kennedy realised that there were many members of the RIC who thought of themselves primarily as Irishmen and who were only too willing to aid the fight for independence. The problem they faced was that the IRA and republican sympathisers actively ostracised RIC members, making it difficult for the RIC men to find someone in the IRA to whom they could pass on information.

Through the Gaelic League, Kennedy was eventually able find a reliable contact in the Kerry RIC: Crimes Special Sergeant Thomas O'Rourke, a man who shared Kennedy's deep love of the Irish language. O'Rourke told Kennedy that he sympathised with the republicans and was willing to help. An initially unsure Kennedy – wary of trusting an RIC man – received personal approval from Collins and began working with O'Rourke.

O'Rourke, in charge of gathering intelligence on the IRA in Kerry, provided invaluable information, including the secret codes used to transmit RIC telegrams. With this code Kennedy was able to decipher intercepted RIC messages and to alert the IRA to all upcoming RIC raids across the country and to all potential IRA suspects the police had identified. This intelligence was gold dust as it allowed Collins, Kennedy and the IRA to stay one step ahead of the RIC for much of the war.

Throughout the war, Kennedy – who spent several months in Dublin working directly for Collins – managed to keep his role as the Kerry IRA Brigade's intelligence officer completely secret. While British forces had successfully identified most of Kerry's leading IRA figures, they never succeeded in identifying the mysterious and highly effective intelligence chief. He kept his role secret by completely ingratiating himself with the RIC and British forces in Kerry.

One story from the days immediately after the Truce of July 1921 sums up how successful Kennedy had been in maintaining the charade. During the war Kennedy had become a close acquaintance of the head of the British Army in Kerry, Colonel Berkley. Kennedy recounts in his BMH testimony, how, after the Truce, he was charged with overseeing the handover of Ballymullen Barracks to the IRA as he was, by then, the Kerry IRA's liaison officer. He stunned Colonel Berkley when he arrived in the barracks and revealed his true role. On seeing him, Kennedy notes, a thoroughly shocked Berkley leapt from his seat and exclaimed, 'Good Christ. I hand it to you people, you're the last man in the world I'd suspect.'

Kennedy, though a supporter of the Treaty, sided with anti-Treaty forces in the Civil War, primarily due to his loyalty to Austin Stack. He was captured by Free State troops in August 1922 and spent approximately six months in prison. He went on to act as Stack's election campaign manager in 1927.

GIRL'S HAIR CUT OFF AT DANCE IN CAHERCIVEEN

Saturday 10 July 1920

At a dance held in the Market, Caherciveen, on Sunday night, a pair of masked men entered the hall, singled out two girls and cut off their hair with scissors. They gave as the reason for their action that the girls were keeping company with soldiers. The raiders got away without any interference from the dancers. The dancing was going on as the operation was carried out.

KENMARE NOTES

Saturday 7 August 1920

On Thursday night the hair was cut off a young lady some distance from the town, and it is rumoured she got several cautions previously against keeping certain company.

YOUNG MAN TAKEN FROM GOLF LINKS AND TARRED

Saturday 11 September 1920

On Wednesday evening, Mr Jas Murphy, son of Mr J. M. Murphy, LL.B. Tralee, was taken from the golf links, Clounalour, where he was engaged in a game of golf, of which he was a well-known exponent, and conveyed by a number of men to the north side of Oakpark, where he was subsequently found tied to a gate and tarred from his waist up.

Mr Murphy was a well-known young man in Tralee. Soon after the outbreak of the recent European War he joined the army and occupied the rank of Second Lieutenant for a number of years. While in France he was wounded and had been out of the army for about two years.

The reasons given for the action taken against Mr Murphy was that he had been negotiating for a cadetship in the R.I.C. some time ago. His assailants had in their possession the correspondence which had passed between Murphy and the Government, which they had read out to him before inflicting the punishment.

TERRORISM IN KERRY
YOUNG MEN ILL-TREATED

Saturday 30 October 1920

(From the 'Irish Independent')

Scenes of terrorism were witnessed in Lixnaw on Sunday at 3 a.m. on the arrival of uniformed men who attempted to burn the Co-operative creamery.

Before entering the village the men, who had their faces blackened and who came in a motor lorry from Ballybunion direction, pulled up at the house of a farmer, Patrick McElligott, who lives half a mile from Lixnaw. When the door was opened, in answer to a loud rapping, inquiries were made if the house were M'Elligott's [*sic*]. His two sons were pulled outside the door in their night attire, and in a downpour of rain they were beaten with the butt end of rifles and kicked. Before leaving, the raiders made them stand for some time in a pool of water almost up to their waists.

The lorry then proceeded to the house of a young man, Stephen Grady, and broke a window. Grady escaped in his night attire through a back window and searchlights were turned upon him but he made good his escape through the fields. His assistant, named Nolan, was knocked unconscious on the floor with the blow of a rifle butt, and subsequently brought outside the door, almost nude, and a tub of water was poured over him. The party then broke into the room where Miss Grady and her mother were sleeping, and pulled Miss Grady out on the road, put her on her knees in a channel of water, and cut her hair.

CREAMERY ATTACKED

By this time the people of the village had awakened, and the raiders were seen taking tins from the lorry and proceeded towards the Co-operative Creamery. Three or four were left on guard at the lorry, while others were posted along the way. The outer door was broken, but the raiders could not get through the second door. The door of the dairy was then wrenched open from the hinges, and the premises were set on fire. Cheese, butter and all the utensils were destroyed as well as a portion of the premises.

On their return from the creamery the raiders entered the house of Maurice Lovett and knocked his son on the floor with a blow of a rifle, and went next door and cut his sister's hair. Before leaving they discharged 4 or 5 shots. The people gathered to the scene of the fire, and succeeded in extinguishing the flames before very much damage was done. The creamery, which was insured against riot to the extent of £25,000, is still working.

Members of the IRA's North Kerry flying column c. 1921.
Front row (left to right): R. Patrick, J. McElligott, Dennis Quille, James Sugrue, Brian Grady.
Middle row: Martin Quille, Christy Brouder, Con Brosnan, Timothy O'Sullivan.
Back row: Dan Grady, Miss M. Aherne, Seán Coughlan. (Courtesy of Mercier Press)

NIGHT OF IRA REPRISALS IN KERRY

Ryle Dwyer

THE War of Independence seemed to come to a head in late October and early November 1920, but events around Tralee, which received extensive international publicity at the time, have been largely overlooked in the history books.

The first official British execution of the conflict took place in Dublin on 1 November 1920, when teenager Kevin Barry was hanged. In the days leading up to the planned execution, the IRA decided to respond by killing as many crown police and soldiers as possible. The order was brought to Kerry No. 1 Brigade by its intelligence officer, Tadhg Kennedy, who was returning to Tralee having spent some months operating with Michael Collins in Dublin.

Attacks on British forces occurred throughout Kerry on 31 October: two Tans were killed in Killorglin, two men were wounded in Dingle, while in Tralee a sailor and a policeman were wounded in ambushes and a further two policemen were taken prisoner and killed, although their bodies have never been found. In Causeway two policemen were wounded, and in Abbeydorney Constable William Madden from County Tipperary was killed and Constable Robert Gorbey was fatally wounded. Three others were shot in Ballyduff, where Constable George Morgan from County Mayo was killed and Constable M. Reidy of County Clare was fatally wounded.

Seven different policemen were ambushed in both Ballybunion and Listowel, but all fourteen escaped uninjured. The same night two Tans were kidnapped by a Ballylongford-based IRA unit in Ballylongford and grossly mistreated during the following days, until the IRA ordered their release. One of those Tans, Constable William Muir from Scotland, never overcame his mistreatment and died by suicide a little over a month later.

Tralee Irish Volunteers, *c.* 1917–18. (Courtesy of Mercier Press)

Paddy Paul Fitzgerald of the Strand Road Company of the IRA was responsible for seizing the two policemen in Tralee. Fitzgerald and seven colleagues had taken up a position that night to ambush a police patrol near the RIC barracks. 'I received word from one of the Fianna that two Tans were standing at the corner of New Road in conversation with two women,' Fitzgerald recalled in his BMH statement. 'Patrick O'Connor and I approached the two Tans with revolvers drawn. I called on them to put up their hands; they complied at once. We took them prisoners and handed them over to a section of our men located near the Dingle–Tralee railway tracks.'

One of those so-called Tans was Constable Patrick Waters, aged twenty-three, a four-year RIC veteran from Loughanbeg, near Spiddal, County Galway.

The other was Constable Ernest Bright, a Londoner in his early thirties. Paddy Cahill, the local IRA brigadier, ordered the execution of the two men that night. The IRA disposed of their bodies, which were never recovered. One story is that the bodies were burned in the furnace of the gas works, but that would have meant bringing them back close to where they were first taken. Fitzgerald, who first took them prisoner, later reportedly said they were buried near 'The Point' at the end of the canal in Blennerville. One of the Fianna scouts involved that night told a similar story, but that area was searched without success.

After I first wrote about this in *The Kerryman* in July 1996 a man told me that his grandfather, William O'Sullivan – who happened to live by the canal, where he was the lock keeper – was an active member of the IRA company that took charge of Waters and Bright. His grandfather's story was that the two men were buried in the O'Sullivan family tomb in Clogherbrien graveyard. When O'Sullivan's wife died in 1926, he balked at burying her with the two policemen, so she was buried beside the family tomb. He was later buried with her. Fanciful stories are often passed down from generation to generation among families, so one has to be careful about what to believe. That grave beside the family tomb, however, lends a degree of circumstantial credence to the story, especially when O'Sullivan was involved in taking custody of the prisoners.

In Tralee the Tans reacted with fury to the events of that day, especially to the news of the two missing policemen. What was to happen in the town during the next nine days, as the Tans tried to secure the return of their police colleagues, made the front pages of newspapers around the world.

THE BATTLE OF TRALEE: TANS RUN AMOK

Ryle Dwyer

IN Tralee, in the early hours of Monday 1 November 1920, the Tans burned down the County Hall, which was opposite the Dominican church. Hearing the news of this, nine international journalists – having the previous day attended the funeral in Cork of Lord Mayor Terence MacSwiney, who had died on a protracted hunger strike – travelled to the town by train to witness what was going on. They included correspondents of the Associated Press of the United States, *Le Journal* (Paris), *The Times*, the *Daily News* and *Evening News*, as well as *The Manchester Guardian*.

Hugh Martin of the *Daily News* had been in Kerry the previous week, reporting on Black and Tan attacks on the creameries in Abbeydorney and Lixnaw. He returned to Kerry with the others. They checked into the Grand Hotel in Denny Street around 9 p.m. A. E. MacGregor, the correspondent of the London-based *Evening News*, decided to walk round the town, and Martin agreed to accompany him. On leaving the hotel they noticed a group of about twenty men standing on the opposite side of the road. 'They were police armed with rifles,' according to Martin.

'What have you come for – to spy on us, I suppose?' one of the men said, before asking what newspapers they represented. The *Evening News* had been favourable to British forces, so MacGregor promptly identified himself, but Martin gave the name of another journalist with a newspaper that supported the British government's Irish policy.

'Is there a Hugh Martin among you?' one of the Tans asked, 'because if there is, we mean to do for him. It's him we want, and we're going to get him.'

MacGregor explained that they had come to Tralee to learn about the burning of the County Hall. The two reporters were told to walk to the corner of the street and read a typewritten notice affixed to the wall. One of the Tans then read out the notice, which Martin took down in shorthand. It read:

Take Notice: Warning!
Unless the two Tralee policemen in Sinn Féin custody are returned before 10 a.m. on the 2nd inst. reprisal of a nature not yet heard of in Ireland will take place in Tralee and surroundings.

'After ten o'clock tomorrow it won't be safe for anybody in Tralee whose face is not known,' one of the Tans warned. Around 11 a.m. the next day Martin learned that word was out that he was in town and he made a hasty retreat to Cork.

'All the afternoon, except for soldiers, the town was as deserted and doleful as if the Angel of Death has passed through it,' Jean de Marsillac of *Le Journal* reported. 'Not a living soul in the streets. All the shops shut and the bolts hastily fastened. All work was suspended, even the local newspapers.'

Martin's report of what had happened to him on Monday evening was published in the *Daily News* on Wednesday and caused an immediate sensation. Questions were asked in the House of Commons about the threat to the reporter. 'There are no steps being taken against journalists in Ireland,' Sir Hamar Greenwood, the chief secretary for Ireland, declared. 'Ireland is the freest country in the world – for journalists.'

The *Sydney Evening News* in Australia reported on its front page on the other side of the world: 'Notices posted in Tralee state that unless two policemen in the custody of Sinn Feiners are released this morning reprisal on a scale unprecedented in Ireland will occur in Tralee. The inhabitants are expecting a night of terror and are fleeing. The shops are shuttered, and the streets deserted.'

On Friday 5 November stories emanating from Tralee were front-page news in *The New York Times*, *New York Tribune* and *Chicago Tribune* in the United States; *The Gazette* (Montreal) and *Calgary Herald* in Canada; as well as the *Sydney*

Evening News. 'I do not remember, even during the war, having seen people so profoundly terrified as those of this little town, Tralee,' wrote de Marsillac. 'The civil authorities are powerless; that there is literally nobody in the world to whom one can appeal, and from whom one can demand protection.'

Saturday was normally the busiest day of the week in Tralee, but nobody was allowed into town. 'Black and Tans take up positions outside bakeries and provision stores where they suspect food could be secured, and at the bayonet's point send famishing women and children from the doors,' *The Freeman's Journal* reported. 'Outside one baker's establishment a Black and Tan, brandishing a revolver, told women and children to clear off, adding "You wanted to starve us, but we will starve you."'

The 'Siege of Tralee' by the Black and Tans was well underway. Montreal's *Gazette* headlined its front-page story that day: 'TRALEE IS PARALYZED: Town Near Starvation and Condition Is Desperate'. The accompanying report described how 'The town of Tralee, Ireland, is fast approaching starvation in consequence of the recent police order forbidding the carrying on of business.' The newspaper concluded that 'the condition of the people is becoming desperate'.

Questions were asked in the House of Commons about events in Tralee on every day on which the Westminster parliament sat during the first half of November. 'There have been many overbearing and merciless chief secretaries but for brazenness, disregard of fact, and economy of truth, Sir Hamar Greenwood remains unsurpassed,' the *Irish Independent* declared in an editorial on 10 November. 'His answers in the House of Commons are the purest travesties.'

'At Tralee the tyranny of an apparently irresponsible police force seems to continue,' *The Times* of London proclaimed.

Tom McEllistrim and his colleagues in the Kerry No. 2 Brigade sought to relieve the pressure on Tralee by striking out at a particular couple of Tans who had been 'giving considerable trouble and terrorising the natives' in the Farranfore area. On 9 November, learning that these two Englishmen had gone to Killarney for the day in civilian clothes, McEllistrim and his colleagues went to Ballybrack, a small railway station between Farranfore and Killarney. When the train from Killarney stopped, they quickly located the two men and shot them dead.

That night in Tralee the announcement was made that the siege would be lifted the next day. That same night at the Guildhall in London, Prime Minister David Lloyd George bragged that the security forces 'had murder by the throat' in Ireland.

What happened in Tralee over these ten days has often been overlooked by historians, probably as a result of the later confusion over the so-called 'Battle of Tralee' the following weekend. On Friday 12 November the Tans raided the creamery in Ballydwyer. When four IRA men bolted from the creamery, the Tans opened fire, killing two – John McMahon and Paddy Herlihy – and wounding two others – Jack McEllistrim and Tim Walsh. They then set fire to the creamery and some nearby homes. Tom McEllistrim and twelve of his men were about a mile away at the time. 'We heard the shooting and saw the lorries depart,' he recalled in his BMH statement. 'We immediately got to the Creamery to assist the wounded.'

Dr Mikey Shanahan was summoned from Tralee. While he was treating the wounded men, those assigned as lookouts were concentrating on the Tralee road and were slow to notice a convoy of cars and trucks approaching from the Castleisland direction. Two Crossley Tender armoured vehicles with Auxiliaries were escorting two cars with officials from Dublin Castle, a film crew, press photographers and an English journalist. They were heading for Tralee.

The first shots fired were really a warning of the approaching danger for those treating the wounded. Seeing men rushing for cover as the convoy approached, the Auxiliaries stopped and opened fire. The cameramen rigged up their movie camera and began recording what, they later claimed, was the first live ambush ever filmed.

Instead of the eight men firing on them, the Auxiliaries estimated there were about seventy in the ambush party. The officer in charge ordered the drivers to turn their vehicles around and they all headed back towards Castleisland.

The next day what was being called the 'Battle of Tralee' made the front page of *The Mail* in Adelaide, Australia. 'The engagement was the fiercest and probably the largest scale of any fight between Crown forces and the Volunteers,' Dublin Castle announced in a press release.

'We had only six rifles in action but two of our party, armed with rifles, who had left the Creamery yard five minutes earlier, came to our aid and opened fire from a little hill on the Auxiliaries at 300 yards range,' McEllistrim explained.

The *Illustrated London News* and a number of British newspapers published what would become an iconic photograph of the struggle. Pathé Gazette prepared a film of the 'Battle of Tralee', but it was promptly exposed as a fake because the whole thing had been embellished with scenes staged on Vico Road in Dalkey, County Dublin. Sir Edward Carson recognised the entrance to his ancestral home there. When the film was shown to a selected audience, one of the men supposedly lying dead on the road gave the whole thing away by getting up before the filming had finished. Hence the film was never released to the general public.

Premises of John R. Walsh burned by the Tans. (Courtesy of Mercier Press)

Following the disclosure of this bogus film, many people apparently thought all the reports about Tralee during the previous week were bogus. What happened may not have been as historically significant as the events of Bloody Sunday in Dublin little over a week later, but the extensive publicity that the actions in Tralee had garnered around the world undoubtedly conditioned the international press to cover the events of Bloody Sunday.

A still from a newsreel film supposedly showing Auxiliaries in action against an IRA column outside Tralee. This scene was actually staged at Vico Road in the leafy and mainly Protestant Killiney suburb of Dublin. (Courtesy of George Morrison)

AUSTIN STACK, MICHAEL COLLINS AND THE WAR OF INDEPENDENCE

Ryle Dwyer

WHEN the Irish Volunteers were organised in Tralee, Austin Stack became the local commander. He was personally informed by Patrick Pearse in February 1916 of the plans for the Easter Rising. Stack was often criticised for his failure to rescue Roger Casement in 1916, but Michael Collins, who later became one of his severest critics, did not blame Stack for this. Indeed, Collins initially admired Stack and confided in him. Some of the best insights into Collins's thinking in 1918 and 1919 can be gleaned from his correspondence with Stack.

'I was very glad to get your letter, especially the personal note which I appreciated,' Collins wrote to Stack on 29 August 1918. 'Without insincerity I can say that I do appreciate it more from yourself than from anyone I know.'

'A' Company, Tralee Battalion, Kerry No. 1 Brigade, IRA. (Courtesy of Mercier Press)

Having helped to spring Éamon de Valera from Lincoln Jail on 3 February 1919, Collins wrote to Stack, who was once again in jail, about plans to confront the British. 'As for us on the outside,' he wrote, 'all ordinary peaceful means are ended and we shall be taking the only alternative actions in a short while now.' Collins thought de Valera would lead a war against the British, but de Valera had other ideas. He believed that diplomatic pressure, not armed conflict, offered the best hope and was planning to go to the United States to get the Americans to put pressure on Britain to recognise Ireland's right to independence.

'The policy now seems to be to squeeze out anyone who is tainted with strong fighting ideas, or should I say the utility of fighting,' Collins wrote to Stack in May. After de Valera went to the United States, Collins set up the 'Squad' and began targeting crown officials, who retaliated, thereby escalating the conflict.

Collins had made arrangements to spring Stack from jail on a number of occasions, but each time Stack had been transferred to another prison before the plans could be implemented. Then, in October 1919, Collins visited Strangeways Prison in Manchester to finalise arrangements for Stack's breakout the following weekend. Stack successfully escaped with five others. He became deputy chief of staff of the IRA following his return to Ireland, but he never attended any meeting of the IRA headquarters staff as he claimed he was too busy working as Minister for Home Affairs after his election in 1918. Within a year of his release Collins was ridiculing Stack as little more than 'a bloody joke' due to his non-attendance of these meetings.

When Collins became acting president of Dáil Éireann, following the arrest of Arthur Griffith in November 1920, de Valera promptly returned to Ireland and tried to send Collins to the United States, but Collins balked: 'That long whoor won't get rid of me as easy as that.' Given de Valera's growing mistrust of Collins, he chose Stack as his deputy president in December 1920.

After a truce was agreed in July 1921, de Valera accepted a British invitation to talks in London to arrange a formal conference. He selected Stack to accompany him, and excluded Collins, who was deeply offended. Kathleen O'Connell, de

Valera's private secretary who hailed from Caherdaniel, noted that Collins 'spent several hours with the President' on the evening of the truce, trying to insist on his inclusion in the delegation.

'Hot discussion,' O'Connell noted in her diary. 'President rather upset.'

Kerry republican leader Austin Stack (*right*) and Éamon de Valera play chess in Arbour Hill Prison, where they were imprisoned in the aftermath of the Civil War.
(Courtesy of George Morrison)

The IRA headquarters staff replaced Stack with Eoin O'Duffy as deputy chief of staff after the Truce came into effect. This was due to Stack's failure to attend any meeting since his appointment as deputy chief of staff in 1919. De Valera tried to re-impose Stack in the hope of controlling Collins's influence over the headquarters staff. At a meeting on 25 November 1921 he proposed Stack's appointment as joint deputy chief of staff, along with O'Duffy, but the other members of the staff wanted nothing to do with Stack and refused to accept the proposal. De Valera became somewhat hysterical, pushing the table in front of him as he jumped to his feet and declaring in a half-scream, 'Ye may mutiny, if ye like, but Ireland will give me another Army.' From this outburst, it appears that signs of an IRA split were already apparent even before the Treaty was agreed.

On the issue of the Treaty, Stack sided with de Valera and seconded his speech denouncing it. He also opposed the subsequent leadership of Griffith and Collins of the Provisional Government. As chairman of the government, Collins appointed former RIC head constable in Tralee John A. Kearney to head a committee to set up An Garda Síochána in February 1922. This was in response to Kearney's role in helping the IRA while serving as an RIC district inspector in Roscommon. But Stack accused Kearney of mistreating Casement. 'This man Kearney was, from my experience of him, one of the most vigilant servants the enemy had in this country, and he did his best – by open means and underhand – to beat us,' Stack complained. He went on to say that Kearney was 'chiefly instrumental in working up a case against Roger Casement'.

This was a contemptible absurdity. Kearney had nothing to do with the 'high treason' conviction for which Casement was executed. Casement had contemplated suicide by poison when he was captured, but abandoned the idea because of the friendliness and compassion shown to him by Kearney. Casement left his watch to Kearney in his will as a token of his gratitude. However, as a married man with ten children, the eldest of whom was only fifteen, Kearney felt compelled by Stack's actions to resign from the new police committee and emigrate for the sake of his family.

Stack's failure to rescue Casement may have been understandable, but his treatment of Kearney, the one person who did help Casement, was utterly reprehensible. If this was Stack's sense of justice, it should hardly be surprising that he left little apparent legacy as Minister for Home Affairs in charge of justice in the revolutionary government of 1919 to 1921.

BATT O'CONNOR: COLLINS'S GENIUS BUILDER

Simon Brouder

ONE Kerryman who played a significant, though less widely known, role in the War of Independence was builder Bartholomew 'Batt' O'Connor (1870–1935), who provided a unique service that helped keep Michael Collins and many other leading rebels out of British hands.

O'Connor – who went on to sit as a TD in Dublin from March 1924 to February 1935 – was born in Brosna in 1870. He grew up there and learned to be a stonemason. At twenty-three he moved to Boston, where he lived for almost five years, before returning to Ireland and moving to Dublin in 1897. Having joined the Gaelic League in 1900, Batt came to know many of the leading figures in the 1916 Rising, including Tom Clarke, Seán Mac Diarmada and Éamon de Valera. O'Connor actually joined the Irish Volunteers in 1913 at the same swearing in ceremony as de Valera.

Though O'Connor wasn't involved in the actual Rising – he was in Kerry at the time – he was still rounded up by the British due to his republican connections and spent several months interned in Frongoch, eventually being released in September 1916. When released he returned to Dublin and re-started his building business while also playing a central role in republican political activities.

O'Connor – who was closely involved with revolutionary Sinn Féin, handling money and hiding sensitive documents for Michael Collins and the leadership – played a key part in the 'National Loan' programme run by Collins. The aim of the loan – which was raised through the sale of bonds to republican supporters in Ireland and the USA – was to fund the First Dáil and the looming War of Independence. It raised an astonishing £400,000 – almost €8,200,000 today –

of which some £250,000 was in gold bars. While the money was easy enough to hide (it was lodged in various bank accounts held by trustees), the gold, a sizeable and extremely heavy cache, was a different proposition.

It was here that O'Connor's building prowess came in especially useful. He built a secret compartment under his house and the gold was safely stashed there until 1922, after the end of the War of Independence.

Collins had long been impressed by O'Connor's building skills and it was with them that the Kerryman made his most unique contribution to the war effort. He was incredibly skilled at creating secret compartments and rooms – hidden using complicated lever and gear systems – which were practically impossible to detect. O'Connor purchased 76 Harcourt Street for Collins. In the house, he installed a secret recess for private papers and a means of escape through the skylight. When the recess escaped discovery following a raid by the army and the DMP, Collins asked him to construct similar hiding places in many of the other houses used by the movement in Dublin. In 5 Mespil Road, Collins's headquarters for over fifteen months during the War of Independence, O'Connor fitted a small cupboard in the woodwork beneath the kitchen stairs on the ground floor where Collins hid his most sensitive papers and files. When the house was finally raided in April 1921, this cupboard too escaped detection.

In one famous incident Collins and Tadhg Kennedy, the Kerry IRA intelligence officer, spent a night in one of O'Connor's hidden rooms in a house on Henry Street in Dublin after the British Army sealed off the entire surrounding area to sweep it for IRA members and sympathisers.

There is little doubt that were it not for O'Connor's building prowess many of the War of Independence leaders may have been captured and so the importance of his work cannot be underestimated.

THE DEFIANT TRALEE DOMINICAN AND THE IRA

Simon Brouder

GIVEN Ireland's staunchly Catholic culture most priests and clerics had nothing to fear from the IRA. However, at the height of the War of Independence, one Tralee-based priest so raised the ire of local republicans that his life was threatened. What is particularly unusual about the incident, however, is the fact that his life wasn't threatened by an IRA member but by one of his own religious superiors.

In 1920 the Dominican Order in Tralee had among its number a former British Army chaplain named Fr Pius. Given his experiences in the trenches of the First World War, Fr Pius had – unlike most other priests in Kerry – little sympathy for the IRA and the struggle for Irish independence. He made no secret of his sympathy for the RIC and the British Army, but it was his support of the Black and Tans that drew the most anger from his congregation and, unsurprisingly, from the Kerry IRA.

From 1920 onwards Intelligence Officer Tadhg Kennedy began receiving reports about Fr Pius's regular visits to the RIC barracks, which were located just a stone's throw from the Dominican church priory. Kennedy and the IRA were told by numerous sources that Fr Pius's visits to the barracks were not in connection with his religious duties and subsequently the IRA approached the priest's superior, Prior Fr Ayers, who was a supporter of the IRA and the independence struggle.

Matters came to a head in April 1921 when the Tralee IRA assassinated the hated Auxiliary officer Major MacKinnon at Oakpark golf course. In the days immediately after MacKinnon's assassination, Fr Pius met a woman outside the Dominican church and in the course of the conversation he condemned the IRA men who had killed the Auxiliary commander. It proved to be a grave mistake on the priest's part for the woman, while extremely devout, was a fervent republican.

Post-war testimony to the BMH by Tadhg Kennedy stated that in reply to Fr Pius's anti-IRA comments she said words to the effect that she 'hoped God would bless the hands of the brave men who shot the tyrant down'. Fr Pius was shocked and incensed and the following Sunday he took to the pulpit to condemn the woman and her comments. As furious and stunned members of the congregation looked on from their pews, Fr Ayer made his way to the altar and had a brief whispered conversation with his cleric. An angered Fr Pius said, 'My superior has forbidden me to preach', and continued with the Mass.

A few days later the home of the woman who was the subject of Fr Pius's pulpit tirade was attacked by Black and Tans, who threw explosives into the building. The woman – whose husband was out at the time – and her child barely escaped with their lives.

The IRA, incensed by the bombing of the woman's home, soon learned that after his controversial sermon had been stopped Fr Pius had reported the entire incident to the Black and Tans and RIC men in the barracks. This was a step too far and the IRA resolved to take action.

Kennedy personally contacted Michael Collins and explained the situation. Collins sent Kennedy to meet with the Dominican superior general in Ireland, Fr Finbar Ryan, to ask that steps be taken to silence the troublesome Fr Pius. After Kennedy explained the situation to Fr Ryan, a second elderly priest, Fr Headley – a former Fenian who was also at the meeting – interjected with a startling question. He bluntly asked Kennedy what the IRA would have done were Fr Pius not a priest. A surprised Kennedy answered that in such circumstances the IRA would have shot the person but given that Fr Pius was a man of the cloth such punishment was not acceptable. Fr Headley's reply – as recounted by Kennedy – was unexpected to say the least. 'You are a brave man and this is no priest of God. Do your duty boy, and you need have no fear of the future,' Fr Headley reportedly said. While the advice was not explicit, Fr Headley's implication was clear. Fr Pius should be shot.

Kennedy and Fr Ryan were stunned and Kennedy immediately assured Fr Ryan that he would allow himself be shot before he would 'do my duty' on a priest, no matter what the situation. Kennedy reported back to Collins, who was equally appalled by the notion of shooting a priest, and a second meeting with Fr Ryan was arranged. At that meeting it was agreed that Fr Ryan would summon Fr Pius to Dublin and offer the politically wayward Tralee-based priest 'some fatherly advice'.

Subsequently Fr Pius was moved to another parish and it was only after the war that he returned to Tralee. He met with Kennedy on his return and expressed his deep regret that his actions had caused such distress to his order and to others. He offered to make amends in any way possible, and so he did. After the war, as Kerry County Council sought damages from the British for the burning of the County Hall during the Siege of Tralee in November 1920, Fr Pius took the stand and gave decisive evidence that it was the Black and Tans and not the IRA who had burned the hall to the ground.

KERRY IN THE
CIVIL WAR

FREE STATE RETAKE KERRY

Simon Brouder

IN the early stages of the Irish Civil War, before the conflict developed into a guerrilla war, the hostilities involved a series of large-scale engagements more typical of regular warfare. One of the most significant of these early engagements came in Kerry in August 1922 as the National Army of the Free State mounted a major offensive to retake the so-called 'Munster Republic'.

The first battle of the Civil War, however, came in Dublin in late June 1922, when the National Army bombarded and retook the Four Courts, which had been in the hands of anti-Treaty forces led by Rory O'Connor since mid-April. O'Connor had served as an intelligence officer at the GPO during the 1916 Rising and been director of engineering for the IRA during the War of Independence. He led that part of the IRA that had refused to accept the Anglo-Irish Treaty of 1921, which established the Irish Free State. On 14 April 1922 O'Connor, with 200 other anti-Treaty IRA men under his command, took over the Four Courts building in the centre of Dublin in defiance of the Provisional Government. They intended to provoke the British troops (who were still in the country) into attacking them, which they thought would restart the war with Britain and re-unite the IRA sides against their common enemy.

The decision to finally attack O'Connor and his men in the court complex – something Michael Collins had wanted to avoid to prevent a full-scale civil war – came in the wake of severe pressure from Winston Churchill and the British government. They assumed that the anti-Treaty IRA was responsible for the assassination of retired British Army Field Marshal Henry Hughes Wilson in London – a killing possibly ordered in secret by Collins – and demanded action be taken against the anti-Treaty forces, particularly those in the Four Courts.

After the Four Courts garrison kidnapped National Army General J. J. O'Connell, Collins and the Free State government took action, delivering an ultimatum to O'Connor and his men to leave the Four Courts and release O'Connell. They refused and the National Army – using British artillery – began the bombardment of the Four Courts, thereby igniting the Civil War. This attack began a week-long battle in Dublin in which Free State troops secured the capital and drove Dublin's anti-Treaty forces out of the city.

With Dublin in pro-Treaty hands, the conflict spread throughout the country. Anti-Treaty forces held Cork, Limerick and Waterford as part of a self-styled independent Munster Republic.

Though much of Munster was in anti-Treaty hands, their forces were not equipped to wage a conventional war and anti-Treaty IRA Chief of Staff Liam Lynch's aim was to hold onto the Munster Republic just long enough to prevent the official foundation of the Free State and to force a renegotiation of the Treaty.

Collins and Richard Mulcahy – the leaders of the Free State government and National Army – felt a quick and decisive victory in Munster was needed if they were to prevent a long and brutal war. So, in July and August they launched an offensive to retake the south and west of the country. Having taken Limerick and Waterford, the Free State forces focused their attention on Cork, Kerry and the west of Ireland. To avoid the hard fighting that would inevitably occur if the army tried to advance overland, it was proposed by Emmet Dalton, a major general in the National Army, that seaborne landings be used. Collins agreed and the army commandeered several civilian passenger ships to transport the troops.

On 2 August the National Army's Dublin Guard landed in Fenit. They were commanded by Brigadier Paddy O'Daly (sometimes referred to as simply Daly), the former leader of Collins's elite assassination unit, the 'Squad', who had led the National Army forces that retook Dublin. Anti-Treaty forces, aware of the dangers of a potential invasion from the seas, had intended to blow up the pier at Fenit if an attack was launched, but the charges were rendered inoperable by unknown persons – thought to most likely have been a disillusioned local anti-Treaty fighter – in an attempt to minimise damage to the port.

With the charges decommissioned, the *Lady Wicklow* had no problem mooring in Fenit and 450 Free State troops were rapidly landed. They quickly made their way into Tralee. The main engagement of the day came at Boherbee, where a large group of anti-Treaty supporters fought the Free State troops in a fierce one-hour firefight. This ferocious battle provided the cover for most of Tralee's anti-Treaty forces to retreat from the town and into the countryside, from where they intended to launch a sustained guerrilla campaign. The Free State troops had landed in Fenit at 10.30 a.m., and by 6 p.m. the town was in Free State hands.

Further landings took place in Tarbert and Kenmare. On 3 August 250 pro-Treaty IRA men from Clare set off in a flotilla of fishing boats and made their

Unable to reach Kerry by road, Irish Free State troops landed at Fenit, Tarbert and Kenmare, and were soon in control of the major towns. (Courtesy of George Morrison)

way across the Shannon Estuary to Tarbert, from where they reinforced the National Army troops. The Free State forces rapidly occupied the towns in the county but the anti-Treaty units in Kerry survived more or less intact and fought a determined guerrilla campaign for the remainder of the war.

The Munster Republic collapsed with the capture of Cork on 10 August. After Cork fell to the Free State, Liam Lynch fled his base in Fermoy and ordered his troops in Munster to stop trying to hold fixed positions and to form flying columns like those that had proved so effective against the British. The Free State

Paddy O'Daly, Eoin O'Duffy and Richard Mulcahy inspecting the Dublin Guard unit of the National Army at Beggars Bush Barracks in January 1922. (Courtesy of Mercier Press)

government's victories in the major towns inaugurated a period of inconclusive guerrilla warfare. Anti-Treaty IRA units held out in areas such as the western part of Counties Cork and Kerry, County Wexford in the east and Counties Sligo and Mayo in the west. Nowhere, however, did the republicans manage to retake any territory lost in the first two months of fighting.

This later guerrilla phase of the war developed into a vicious cycle of revenge killings and reprisals as the anti-Treaty forces assassinated pro-Treaty politicians and the Free State responded with the execution of prisoners. In Kerry the cycle of reprisals was particularly brutal and Paddy O'Daly's forces acted with particular viciousness in the county. As the Civil War dragged on his men were implicated in a series of atrocities against anti-Treaty prisoners, culminating in the killings of March 1923, the most famous of which took place in Ballyseedy outside Tralee, where prisoners were killed with landmines. Questioned about the brutal tactics of his troops, O'Daly – who said those killed in Ballyseedy, Countess Bridge and Cahersiveen were accidentally blown up by their own mines – was unrepentant. 'Nobody asked me to take kid-gloves to Kerry, so I didn't,' he said.

Republican forces burn Tralee's former RIC barracks in the face of the National Army's advance. (Courtesy of Deirdre O'Sullivan)

STIFF RESISTANCE

(article from *The Freeman's Journal*)

Monday 7 August 1922

TRALEE CAPTURED AFTER HEAVY FIGHTING

A despatch to hand from the OC troops in the Kerry areas says:–

'We landed at Fenit on Wednesday morning.

'Fire was opened on us from the Coastguard Station and from other posts along the beach. Our troops landed successfully and rushed the village.

'We suffered two casualties … The Irregulars retreated before our fire and were closely pursued by the men of the Dublin Guards. We overtook them at Spa, where after a bitter engagement, the Irregulars were again forced to retreat, leaving behind them one dead, one wounded and 6 prisoners. Our losses were Volunteer Byrne (killed) and Lieut. Mtn. Nolan (slightly wounded).

'We divided forces at Spa. Comdt. McGuinness and Vice-Comdt. Dempsey, with one party, pushed on towards Tralee. Capt. MacLean, with another party, advanced along the coast to enter the town …

'The first of our troops entered Tralee at 1.30 p.m. by Pembroke Street. They rushed Rock Street from this point and it immediately fell into our hands. At the same time Commandant Dempsey encircled the town, whilst Commandant McGuinness forcing his way via Boherbee, took possession of the Staff Barracks.

HEAVY FIGHTING

'A fierce engagement, lasting over an hour, took place here. A large body of the Irregulars evacuated Ballymullen Barracks and set fire to the building before they left, but a large portion of the building was saved by the troops. The police barracks in Church Street was also set on fire by the Irregulars before they left.

'The town was completely in our hands at 6 p.m.

During the assault at Rock street one soldier was wounded. The Red Cross men immediately started to his assistance, carrying two large Red Cross flags and stretchers.

'Fire was opened on them from the police barrack, and Volunteer Harding was shot dead and Volunteer Fleming was wounded …

'This cowardly act was witnessed by a large number of townspeople, who were loud in their condemnation of such a despicable act.'

Free State soldiers securing Listowel from republican forces. (Courtesy of Mercier Press)

TWO WEEKS OF BLOODY MASSACRES

Ryle Dwyer

ON 6 March 1923 Lieutenant Paddy O'Connor of the Free State was lured into Ballanarig Wood near Knocknagoshel with information about an IRA dugout and was decapitated by the mine which had been planted there by the IRA. Four of his colleagues were also killed: Captains Michael Dunne and Joseph Stapleton of the Dublin Brigade, and Privates Michael Galvin of Killarney and Laurence O'Connor of Causeway. Another colleague lost both legs as a result of the explosion. The Free State troops retaliated with fury, killing no less than nineteen republican prisoners in Kerry within the next two weeks. Dunne and Stapleton had served in the famous 'Squad' with Paddy O'Daly, who was now in charge of the Kerry Command.

'In the event of encountering any obstacles, such as stone barricades,' O'Daly ordered, precautions should be taken. 'The officer or NCO in charge should immediately proceed to the nearest Detention barracks and bring with him a sufficient number of irregular prisoners to remove same,' he ordered.' The tragedy of Knocknagoshel must not be repeated and serious disciplinary action will be taken against any officer who endangers the lives of his men in the removal of such barricades.'

However, O'Daly was not about to wait for IRA prisoners to be killed moving booby-trapped barricades. With his full knowledge and approval, a mine was constructed by Captains Ed Flood and Jim Clarke in Tralee and placed in a pile of stones in the middle of the road at Ballyseedy Cross, a little over three miles from Tralee. Nine republican prisoners were selected at Ballymullen Barracks in Tralee. The only criterion for their selection was that none should be closely related to any priests or nuns. Colonel David Neligan selected the men and picked John Daly, Michael O'Connell and Patrick Buckley of Castleisland; Stephen Fuller, George O'Shea and Tim Tuomey of Kilflynn; Patrick Hartnett of Finuge; James Walsh of Churchill; and John O'Connor from Waterford.

The men were taken to Ballyseedy in an army truck. On the way Commandant Ned Breslin of Donegal offered them a cigarette each, saying it would be 'the last you'll have'. He told them they were going to be blown up just like the Free State soldiers killed at Knocknagoshel. On several occasions in recent days the men had been taken out and told they were going to be shot, but each time they were brought back again. This time they were ordered to stand around a pile of rocks in which a mine had been placed earlier.

'They then came round the front of us and tied our ankles and knees,' according to Stephen Fuller. 'One fellow asked to be let say his prayers and the fellow who was tying him hit him on the top of the head with the rope and said "no prayers". Just like children we did as we were told and no more,' Fuller said.

'Some of you fellows might go to Heaven, if you do you can say hello to our boys,' the soldier added.

The military moved away about 150 yards. 'You can be praying away as long as you like,' an officer told them.

'I kept my eyes on him all the time,' Fuller added, 'and it wasn't until the fellow beside me started saying his prayers that I thought of saying mine. I said "goodbye" and George O'Shea said, "Goodbye, goodbye, lads". Then the mine went off.'

By some explosive freak, Fuller was blown clear and found himself by the roadside. 'I made for the ditch,' he said. He slipped across a shallow river. At that point the soldiers opened rapid fire with a machine gun to kill the wounded. 'I thought they were firing at me and I ran until I met another fence and met the gable of a house,' he recalled. The house was the Currans' at Hanlon's Cross, where he found shelter. The bodies of the dead were so mutilated that the military did not realise in the falling darkness that they had not killed all of the men.

The same day as the Ballyseedy massacre there was a comparatively similar incident at Countess Bridge near Killarney. Jer O'Donoghue, Stephen Buckley, Daniel O'Donoghue, Tim Murphy and Tadhg Coffey had been taken from jail to the bridge by Free State forces. There was a low barricade of stones across the road and they were ordered to move them out of the way. As they were moving the stones the mine went off. When Coffey looked up he could see Murphy, Buckley and Dan O'Donoghue covered with blood, moaning and moving on the ground. They were not dead, but grenade after grenade was thrown among them and shots were fired. Amid the confusion, Coffey made it to the adjacent woods and – like Stephen Fuller at Ballyseedy – escaped unnoticed.

Five days later, in Cahersiveen, the Free State troops made sure that none of the five men that they took from Cahersiveen to nearby Bahaghs would be able to escape, because they shot each man in the legs before laying them over a landmine and blowing them up. On this occasion, however, one of the Free State soldiers, Lieutenant W. McCarthy, was so revolted that he publicised the story. 'There were six or eight in the lot that murdered them,' McCarthy said. 'It was a murder gang that is going around trying to keep on the war. We ourselves will support the Free State government and fight for it, but we will not fight for murder.'

Richard Mulcahy had persuaded the Dáil to make the unauthorised possession of a firearm a capital offence to prevent soldiers taking the law into their own hands, but they were doing it anyway and the government was turning the proverbial blind eye. Captain Niall Harrington, a Tralee man serving in the National Army, was so disgusted with the conduct of his fellow soldiers that he prepared his own report for Minister for Justice Kevin O'Higgins. 'The mines used in the slaughter of the prisoners were constructed in Tralee under the supervision of two senior Dublin Guards officers,' he reported. Having sent this report, he feared for his own life and asked to be transferred out of Kerry. When he was instead moved to Tralee, Harrington feared the worst and spent a night in Benners Hotel in an armchair facing the door with two loaded pistols at the ready.

But the whole thing appears to have been a clerical error and word of his transfer up the country came through the following day.

Following the disclosure of Fuller's story, Minister for Defence Richard Mulcahy ordered an army inquiry, but this was never going to be anything other than the proverbial whitewash. He selected Major General Paddy O'Daly – the man who was essentially behind the whole thing – to preside at the inquiry, along with one of his own officers, Colonel J. McGuinness, and Major General Éamonn (Bob) Price from headquarters. The inquiry proved to be a monumental charade. One officer testified that he was bringing a message to Killorglin when he came across the barricade, so he returned to Ballymullen Barracks to get some prisoners to clear the road, in line with O'Daly's orders. Commandant Breslin then testified that he delivered nine prisoners to Ballyseedy:

> I got the prisoners out of the truck, lined them up, told them what I had brought them there for, and instructed them to remove the barricade which they proceeded to do. I inspected the barricade myself. I became suspicious and asked my men to move back. The prisoners were at work on the barricade for a couple of minutes when I heard a very loud explosion. For a few minutes after that I was knocked to the ground. When I got up I found that the bodies had been scattered on the road.

It was a tissue of lies. There was no mention of the machine gun opening up to ensure that all the men were killed. If the government had been remotely interested in the truth, it would have only had to examine the mutilated bodies to find the bullet wounds.

So many people were being killed in military custody in Kerry that the army issued orders on 21 March 1923 that henceforth 'prisoners who die while in military custody in the Kerry Command shall be interred by the troops in the area in which the death has taken place'. This was tantamount to approving the barbarity and merely telling the soldiers to cover up their vile deeds properly.

Maurice Riordan of Waterville made a claim for compensation for the death of his son, who had been arrested as part of an IRA armed column on 2 March 1923 during the Civil War. Éamonn Coogan, the deputy commissioner of An Garda Síochána, reported that Riordan was one of the prisoners taken from the workhouse in Cahersiveen. 'The five prisoners were subsequently shot and their bodies blown up by a mine at Bahaghs,' Coogan wrote. 'Evidence of these facts can be procured.'

Neither Captain Harrington nor Lieutenant McCarthy were called to testify in the inquiry. 'The evidence taken at the Court of Enquiry,' Henry O'Friel, the secretary of the Department of Justice reported to Kevin O'Higgins on 8 January 1924, 'can scarcely be regarded as having in all the circumstances much value.' O'Friel favoured either bringing charges against the army personnel involved, or at least having 'a full investigation into the episode at which all available witnesses would be present and properly examined'. But the Free State cabinet decided on 22 January 1924:

> that prima facia evidence of complicity in an attack against the State on the part of an applicant for compensation or of the reason in respect of whom compensation is claimed is a bar to the claim. The onus of preparing evidence in respect of any alleged excesses by the troops during the period of hostility rests upon the party who considers himself aggrieved.

'The Government decision may be taken as covering all cases of prisoners whose deaths were caused by mine explosion at Ballyseedy Bridge, near Tralee, Countess Bridge near Killarney and Baghas Bridge near Caherciveen,' O'Friel informed the secretary of the Compensation Committee.

Others filed for compensation, but met with the same government indifference. Patrick Buckley, who was killed in the Ballyseedy massacre, had a wife and six children. 'They have no visible means of obtaining a livelihood,' Deputy Commissioner Coogan wrote. But the Compensation Committee could not have cared less. The secretary of the committee reported that he and his colleagues 'will be very careful to guard against making any recommendation for payment of compensation when there has been any "default" on the part of the applicant or the person injured'. If the British had behaved that way, we would never have heard the end of it!

GOVERNMENT DENIES REPORTS OF ATROCITIES IN TROOPS IN KERRY

(article from the *Irish Independent*)

Monday 19 March 1923

The Free State Army has issued the following statement in response to stories of an atrocity committed at Ballyseedy near Tralee on 7th March.

'A party of troops proceeding from Tralee to Killorglin last night came across a barricade of stones built on the roadway at Ballyseedy Bridge.

'The troops returned to Tralee and brought out a number of prisoners to remove the obstruction.

'While engaged in this work a trigger mine (which was concealed in the structure) exploded, wounding Captain Edward Breslin, Lieutenant Joseph Murragh and Sergeant Ennis, and killed eight of the prisoners.'

However, a different version of events is in circulation through the county, where it is said that nine Republican prisoners were taken from Ballymullen Barracks, Tralee, on 7th March, and tied in a circle around a landmine placed by National Troops, which was then detonated.

One of the prisoners, Stephen Fuller, was miraculously blown clear in the explosion and is now on the run.

The deaths at Ballyseedy occur in the aftermath of the Irregulars' killing of five National Troops in an explosion near Knocknagoshel on March 6th.

And a further atrocity is reported from the Countess Bridge, near Killarney, where four Republican prisoners were ordered to remove a barricade of stones which had been built across the road. A mine exploded as they did so, wounding the men.

Grenades were then thrown by Free State troops and shots were fired.

One of the prisoners, Tadhg Coffey, is reported to have escaped in the midst of the confusion.

And in Caherciveen on March 12th, five Irregulars died in a land-mine explosion in similar circumstances.

The coffins containing the bodies of those who died at Ballyseedy were handed over to relatives by National Troops outside the Barrack gates, Tralee.

The relatives removed the remains in the public street from coffins supplied by the military and transferred them to other coffins. Military coffins were then broken up and left lying on the roadway.

Eleven members of Kerry County Council have resigned in protest at these events. In a letter to the *Cork Weekly Examiner* they stated:

> We, the undersigned members of Kerry County Council, now resign until a guarantee will be given that no further executions will take place, and that prisoners will be given prisoner-of-war treatment.

Rural District Councils in Killarney and Millstreet have also resigned. General Richard Mulcahy, Commander in Chief, Free State Army, denied that any such actions had taken place and defended the army in the Dáil:

> These officers have my fullest confidence, and I believe that the honour of the Army is as dearly rooted in them as it is in us here, or in any member of the Government.

THE KERRY GAA AND RECONCILIATION

Ryle Dwyer

THE Irish Civil War was at its bitterest in Kerry, where the worst atrocities of the conflict occurred at Ballyseedy, Countess Bridge and Cahersiveen in March 1923. Those atrocities engendered enormous bitterness that took years to overcome, but there can be no doubt that Gaelic football played a major role in the healing process. Players who had fought on both sides of the Civil War came together on the Kerry team, with the result that people from across the political divide could unite in supporting the team. This, in turn, played a major role in bringing the people of the county together.

Dublin won the first three All-Ireland football championships concluded after the Civil War. Those included the unfinished championships of 1921 and 1922 – the finals of which were both played in 1923. Dublin went on to beat Kerry in the All-Ireland final of 1923, played on 28 September 1924. The Kerry team that played that day included Con Brosnan, who had been a captain in the National Army. He managed to ensure safe passage to games for republican players like John Joe Sheehy and Joe Barrett. Sheehy went on to captain Kerry to All-Ireland victories in 1926 and 1930, while Brosnan and Barrett went on to win six All-Ireland medals each over the next eight years.

Having won the championships of 1924 and 1926, Kerry won again in 1929 with Joe Barrett as captain. He was selected as captain again in 1931 when Kerry was going for its first three-in-a-row. In a magnificent sporting gesture, Barrett handed the captaincy to Con Brosnan in recognition of his role in putting the game above politics. Although Barrett's club mate J. J. 'Purty' Landers – a life-long republican – was passed over for the captaincy, he warmly endorsed the gesture towards Brosnan. 'Regardless of pressure from within his own side of the divide, or from the other side,' Landers said, 'he [Brosnan] did what he believed had to be done to bring about peace and healing.'

Brosnan went on to lift the Sam Maguire Cup in September 1931, thereby embellishing the magnificent example of sportsmanship. Kerry made it four-in-a-row the following year, with Barrett as captain for a second time.

The key to the passionate support for Gaelic football in Kerry undoubtedly owes a great deal to the role that football played in bringing the people of the county together amidst the bitterness engendered by the Civil War.

JOHN JOE SHEEHY

Simon Brouder

ONE of the best known Kerry figures in the War of Independence, John Joe Sheehy (1897–1980), commanded the Boherbee Company of the IRA and later took control of the Tralee Battalion. Sheehy, like most IRA members in Kerry, sided against the Anglo-Irish Treaty in 1922.

During the Civil War when Free State troops landed in Kerry as part of a seaborne offensive, he was in command of the anti-Treaty garrison in Tralee. After the Free Staters took the town, Sheehy retreated and, as the conflict became a guerrilla war, he found himself in charge of three columns of around seventy-five men in the Ballymacthomas area.

Sheehy was a comrade of Tom McEllistrim during the Civil War and in January 1923 the pair led a republican mortar attack on the National Army barracks in Castlemaine.

Just after the Civil War, when Sheehy was still on the run, he famously managed to play football for Kerry as the then Kerry captain Con Brosnan, though a member of the National Army, guaranteed his safe passage. In order to appear at the games, Sheehy paid into the Munster and All-Ireland finals, slipped off his street clothes and played. At the final whistle, he disappeared back into the crowd. He was a member of the Kerry senior inter-county team from 1919 until 1930 and captained Kerry to the All-Ireland title in 1926 and again in 1930.

APPENDIX 1

Easter Rising timeline with special reference to Kerry

Compiled by Ryle Dwyer

25 Nov. 1913	Irish Volunteer Force (IVF) formed at the Rotunda, Dublin.
10 Dec. 1913	Meeting to establish the Irish Volunteers in Tralee.
18 Jan. 1914	IVF formed in Cahersiveen.
5 Apr. 1914	IVF formed in Castleisland.
1 May 1914	IVF formed in Currans.
16 May 1914	IVF formed in Ballymacelligott.
30 May 1914	IVF formed in Knocknagoshel.
31 May 1914	IVF formed in Killorglin.
6 June 1914	IVF formed in Ventry.
7 June 1914	IVF formed in Scartaglin.
8 June 1914	IVF formed in Keel.
13 June 1914	IVF formed in Lixnaw.
14 June 1914	Parade of IVF in Tralee.
28 June 1914	Patrick Pearse inspects the IVF in Ardfert.
	Ballybunion Volunteers formed at Doon.
25 July 1914	IVF set up in Glenbeigh.
26 July 1914	Howth gun-running.
20 Sept. 1914	John Redmond's speech at Woodenbridge, Co. Wicklow, urging Volunteers to join the British war effort.
24 Sept. 1914	Eoin MacNeill calls on the IVF to reject Redmond's call.
13 Oct. 1914	Tralee Volunteers vote to support MacNeill.
18 Oct. 1914	National Volunteers formed in Tralee.
19 Oct. 1914	Cahersiveen Volunteers side with MacNeill.
	IVF reorganised in Abbeydorney.
21 Nov. 1914	County convention of IVF.
23 May 1915	MacNeill reviews IVF at Killarney.
1 Aug. 1915	IVF parades in Tralee to mark O'Donovan Rossa's funeral.
26 Feb. 1916	Pearse meets Irish Volunteers in Tralee.
9 Apr. 1916	*Aud* leaves Lübeck en route to Ireland.

12 Apr. 1916	Roger Casement, Robert Monteith and Daniel Bailey board U-20 at Wilhelmshaven.
14 Apr. 1916	Germans told not to land arms until Easter Sunday.
15 Apr. 1916	Franz von Papen sends a wireless message from New York to Boston about delivery dates of arms to Fenit.
18 Apr. 1916	US Secret Service seize the message and pass it to the British.
20 Apr. 1916	*Aud* arrives in Tralee Bay.
21 Apr. 1916	Roger Casement arrested near Banna.
	Austin Stack arrested in Tralee.
	Drownings at Ballykissane Pier.
22 Apr. 1916	*Aud* intercepted and scuttled off the coast of Cork.
	Daniel Bailey arrested in Abbeydorney.
	MacNeill publishes countermanding order, calling off Rising.
23 Apr. 1916	Word reaches Tralee that the Rising has been cancelled.
	Casement interrogated in London.
	IRB reorganises the Rising for Easter Monday.
24 Apr. 1916	Easter Rising begins in Dublin.
28 Apr. 1916	Michael J. O'Rahilly (Ballylongford), Michael Mulvihill (Ardoughter, Ballyduff), Patrick Shortis (Ballybunion) and Patrick O'Connor (Rathmore) killed in Dublin.
30 Apr. 1916	Thomas Ashe, Lispole, is the last commandant to surrender.
5 May 1916	Tralee Urban District Council 'deplores' the Easter Rising.
8 May 1916	Ashe sentenced to death by military court; sentence then commuted to life in prison.
12 May 1916	Prime Minister Herbert H. Asquith arrives in Dublin.
23 May 1916	Nineteen Kerry prisoners deported to internment in Britain.
29 May 1916	Two RIC constables shot in Firies.
29 June 1916	Casement found guilty of high treason and sentenced to death.
9 July 1916	Kerry MPs M. J. Flavin and T. O'Sullivan visit Kerry prisoners in Wales.
20 July 1916	Fifteen Kerry prisoners released from Frongoch Internment Camp, Wales.
29 July 1916	US Senate adopts resolution calling for clemency for Irish prisoners.
1 Aug. 1916	Dick Fitzgerald (Killarney) and M. J. Moriarty (Dingle) released from Frongoch.
3 Aug. 1916	Casement executed.
22 Dec. 1916	All remaining Kerry internees released from Frongoch.

APPENDIX 2

Casement Timeline

Compiled by Ryle Dwyer

1864   Roger David Casement born.

1873   Anne Jephson (mother) dies.

1877   Captain Roger Casement (father) dies.
       Casement raised by his uncle John Casement (Magherintemple, Ballycastle, County Antrim) and educated as a boarder at Ballymena Diocesan School.

1880   Clerical job with Elder Dempster, a Liverpool shipping company.

1892   Joins the British Colonial Service.

1895   Appointed British consul for Mozambique.

1898   Appointed British consul for Angola.

1901   Appointed British consul for the eastern part of French Congo.

1903   Commissioned by the British government to investigate the human rights situation in the Congo Free State.

1904   Publication of the Casement Report, instrumental in King Leopold of Belgium relinquishing his personal holdings in Africa.
       Joins Conradh na Gaeilge/Gaelic League.

1905   Appointed Companion of the Order of St Michael and St George (CMG) for his Congo work.
       Joins Sinn Féin.

1906   Sent to Brazil, first as consul in Pará, then transferred to Santos. Later promoted to consul-general in Rio de Janeiro.

1910 & 1911   Pays two visits to the Putumayo Indians.

1911   Details the rubber companies' mistreatment of the Putumayo Indians and is knighted for his efforts on behalf of the Amazonian Indians.

1913   Retires from British Colonial Service.

1914   (July) Finances and organises the Howth gun-running. Travels to the USA to promote and raise money for the Volunteers.
       (August) Meets with John Devoy and Count Bernstorff, a top-ranking German diplomat, to propose a mutually beneficial plan in New York.

(October) Sails to Germany.

(November) Negotiates a declaration by Germany not to invade Ireland and recruits prisoners of war to the Irish Brigade.

1916 (April) Germany offers 20,000 Mosin–Nagant 1891 rifles, ten machine guns and accompanying ammunition.

(21 April) Lands at Banna Strand, Tralee Bay, County Kerry and is later arrested.

(26 June) Trial begins in London.

(29 June) Found guilty of high treason.

(30 June) Knighthood revoked in the Court of Criminal Appeal, London.

(18 July) Appeal denied.

(3 August) Hanged by John Ellis at Pentonville Prison (London).

1917 First anniversary of execution marked by a great public gathering at McKenna's Fort near Ardfert. Fort renamed Casement's Fort. Thomas Ashe delivers the oration.

1929 Lengthy negotiations between the Irish and British governments for repatriation of Casement's remains begin.

1953 Casement Park, Belfast, opened.

1959 Casement diaries declassified at British National Archives (Kew).

1965 State funeral of Sir Roger Casement in Dublin.

1966 Plaque to commemorate Casement's memory unveiled at Tralee train station, after whom the station is renamed.

1968 Unveiling of the Casement Memorial at Banna Strand.

1978 Gaelscoil Mhic Easmainn, Tralee, founded by Conradh na Gaeilge.

APPENDIX 3

War of Independence timeline of events in Kerry

Compiled by Ryle Dwyer

1918

13 Apr.	Raid on Gortatlea Barracks for arms. Two Volunteers killed.
17 Apr.	Monster rally against conscription in Tralee.
14 June	Sergeant Boyle and Constable Fallon ambushed in Tralee.
5 July	All public gatherings banned in Ireland.
18 Dec.	Sergeant Patrick Maloney shot and wounded in Annascaul.

1919

21 Jan.	Dáil Éireann established.
6 Feb.	De Valera escapes from Lincoln Jail.
24 June	RIC ambushed and disarmed near Camp.
25 Oct.	Austin Stack escapes from Strangeways Prison.
2 Nov.	Detective Sergeant Thomas Wharton of Killarney shot by the IRA in Dublin.
30 Nov.	Detective Sergeant John Barton of Ballymacelligott shot by the IRA in Dublin.
24 Dec.	Constable Maurice Keogh of Limerick accidently shot by a colleague in Killarney.

1920

3 Jan.	Constable Clarke shot and wounded by the IRA in Ballylongford.
13 Feb.	Volunteer John Heaphey shot in Ballylongford by the RIC.
19 Feb.	Sergeant McDonagh and Constables Fagan and Dunphy wounded in an attack on RIC barracks in Camp.
8 Mar.	Three RIC men disarmed at Ballyronan, near Ballyheigue.
10 Mar.	Detective Sergeant George Neazer shot dead in Rathkeale by the IRA.
12 Mar.	Ballybunion Barracks attacked.
16 Mar.	Cornelius Kelly, courthouse caretaker, shot dead by the IRA in Caherdaniel.
25 Mar.	Gortatlea police hut burned out.

30 Mar.	Constable Flaherty of Cloghane wounded and Constables Lavelle and Darlington overpowered and disarmed at Stradbally, near Castlegregory.
31 Mar.	Scartaglin RIC Barracks attacked by the IRA.
2 Apr.	RIC patrol disarmed at Causeway.
3 Apr.	Abandoned RIC barracks burned down in Ardfert, Ballyheigue, Ardea, Lauragh, Templenoe, Mulgrave, Headford and Beaufort.
	Customs House and offices of tax collectors sacked in Tralee.
4 Apr.	Vacant RIC barracks burned out in Ballinaskelligs.
	RIC accused of breaking windows in Tralee.
5 Apr.	Vacant RIC barracks burned at Newtownsandes (modern-day Moyvane).
6 Apr.	Vacant RIC barracks in Cordal and Scartaglin destroyed.
10 Apr.	Fr William Ferris threatened with death in Tralee.
17 Apr.	Constable Martin Clifford killed at Bradley's Cross near Waterville by the IRA.
18 Apr.	Courthouse burned in Dingle.
21 Apr.	Constable Patrick Foley of Annascaul kidnapped by the IRA near home.
23 Apr.	Constable Foley's body found with twenty-six bullet wounds at Deelis.
25 Apr.	Sergeant Cornelius Crean of Annascaul killed in Ballinspittle.
27 Apr.	Three RIC men held up in Annascaul. Constable MacPherson wounded.
30 Apr.	Military supplies burned in Dingle rail yard.
3 May	Sergeant Francis J. McKenna shot dead near Listowel.
4 May	RIC break windows in Tralee.
7 May	D. J. O'Sullivan, chairman of Tralee Urban District Council, released from Wormwood Scrubs Prison in London after fourteen days on hunger strike.
10 May	Volunteers Dan Healy of Tralee and Alexander O'Donnell of Castlegregory released from Wormwood Scrubs while on hunger strike.
	Constable William Brick from Tralee killed in Timoleague.
14 May	Four cannons taken from Ross Castle by the IRA.
15 May	Vacant RIC barracks at Lixnaw burned.
23 May	Brandon coastguard station burned down.
26 May	Attack on a Black and Tan contingent by the IRA at Glenbeigh.
28 May	Volunteer Liam Scully of Glencar killed in attack on Kilmallock RIC Barracks.
31 May	Private Miller shot dead accidentally in Dingle coastguard station.
2 June	Fenit RIC Barracks attacked. Sergeant Murphy and Constable O'Regan wounded.

3 June	G. B. F. Smyth appointed divisional commissioner of RIC for Munster.
5 June	Newtownsandes Barracks burned.
	Military patrol attacked near Newtownsandes.
	Plan to burn Brosna RIC Barracks foiled by the military.
9 June	Fenit coastguard station attacked.
11 June	Army petrol consignment seized by the IRA in Tralee.
18 June	Brosna Barracks attacked.
19 June	Army heading for Brosna attacked near Castleisland.
	RIC mutiny in Listowel.
28 June	Constable Rael wounded near his home in Ardfert.
11 July	IRA attack on Rathmore Barracks; Constable Alexander Will killed.
	IRA attack on Farranfore RIC Barracks.
13 July	Constables Michael Lenihan and George Roche killed in an ambush en route from Cloghane to Dingle. District Inspector Michael Fallon wounded.
16 July	Constables Cooney and Clear wounded in the Glencar Ambush.
18 July	RIC Divisional Commissioner G. B. F. Smyth shot dead in Cork city.
20 July	Surprise attack by the IRA from a train in Tralee.
26 July	Two RIC constables wounded in Lixnaw.
2 Aug.	Cloghane RIC Barracks burned.
13 Aug.	Two RIC wounded in an IRA attack between Abbeydorney and Tralee.
14 Aug.	Military stores burned at railway yard in Tralee.
	Police burn printing works of *Kerry News*, *Kerry Weekly Reporter* and *Killarney Echo* in Russell Street, Tralee.
18 Aug.	Military escort disarmed near Annascaul.
19 Aug.	Volunteer Paddy Kennedy of Annascaul killed.
21 Aug.	Sergeant Dan Maunsell of Ballyheigue killed in Inchigeela, County Cork.
	Constable John O'Hanlon of Kerry killed in Kilrush.
28 Aug.	Raids for shotguns in Cahersiveen.
1 Sept.	Attack on Cashen Pier coastguard station.
11 Sept.	Former soldier James Murphy tarred at the golf links in Tralee.
12 Sept.	Lixnaw creamery raided by the RIC.
14 Sept.	Constables Prior, Lavelle and Holmes wounded going to Causeway.
15 Sept.	Mail robbed from the train at Headford.
17 Oct.	Tralee shot up by Black and Tans.

18 Oct.	Abbeydorney creamery burned by Black and Tans.
	Vacated RIC Barracks at Anabeg, near Lixnaw, burned out by the IRA.
	Sinn Féin Hall at Finuge burned by Black and Tans.
	Military stores at Tralee railway station raided by the IRA.
31 Oct.	Constables William Madden, Robert Gorbey and George Morgan fatally wounded in Ballyduff.
	Two military police wounded in Green Street, Dingle.
	Constables Herbert Evans and Albert Caseley killed near Killorglin.
	Constables Patrick Waters and Ernest Bright killed in Tralee.
	Constable Daniel McCarthy shot through the knee in Tralee.
	Sailor Bert S. Woodward wounded in Tralee.
1 Nov.	Siege of Tralee begins.
	Creamery and seven homes burned by Tans in the Abbeydorney area.
	John Houlihan, a teenager, killed by Tans near Ballyduff because his brother was a known Volunteer.
	Tans burn buildings in Killorglin and shoot W. M. O'Sullivan.
	Constables James Coughlan and William Muir kidnapped in Ballylongford.
2 Nov.	Volunteer Tommy Wall shot dead in Tralee.
4 Nov.	Questions asked in Westminster parliament about the threat to journalist Hugh Martin in Tralee.
5 Nov.	Ardfert Creamery sacked by Black and Tans.
	M. Maguire of Ardfert killed.
	Seven civilians reported killed in Causeway.
	Tralee siege news makes the front page of *The Gazette* in Montreal and *The New York Times*.
6 Nov.	T. Archer killed in Kilflynn.
8 Nov.	Volunteers M. Brosnan of Castleisland and J. Cantillon of West Commons, killed in Ardfert.
	Report from Tralee again on the front pages of *The Gazette* in Montreal and *The New York Times*.
	Prime Minister David Lloyd George says he has 'murder by the throat' in Ireland.
	Two Black and Tan constables killed at Ballybrack.
10 Nov.	Siege of Tralee lifted.

10 Nov.	Frank Hoffman killed by Black and Tans at Farmer's Bridge.
11 Nov.	Constable Whippen shot and wounded in Castleisland.
12 Nov.	Ballymacelligott creamery sacked and press supposedly ambushed.
	P. Herlihy and J. McMahon of Ballymacelligott killed.
22 Nov.	Volunteer Eddie Carmody killed in Ballylongford.
26 Nov.	Soldier shot and wounded outside the library in Castleisland.
2 Dec.	Uniformed men smash windows in Killarney.
20 Dec.	Bishop Coughlan of Cork orders the excommunication of anyone who organises an ambush.
24 Dec.	Andrew Moynihan of Rathmore killed by Auxiliaries.
25 Dec.	John Leen and Maurice Reidy killed in Ballymacelligott.
26 Dec.	J. Hickey of Knocknagoshel killed.
27 Dec.	Constable William Muir of Edinburgh commits suicide in Ballylongford.
	J. Hackett of Ballylongford killed.

1921

1 Jan.	J. Lawlor, a clerical student, killed in Listowel.
11 Jan.	Auxiliaries round up men in Tralee.
20 Jan.	District Inspector Tobias O'Sullivan shot in Listowel.
23 Jan.	Round-up in Ballymacelligott by British forces.
	Constable Timothy Keane of Kerry killed in Tipperary.
26 Jan.	Cadet Charles Englesden killed accidently in Listowel.
28 Jan.	Divisional Commander Philip A. Holmes and Constable Thomas Moyles of Mayo killed at Toureengarriffe, seven miles from Castleisland.
	Volunteer Bob Browne killed in Fealsbridge.
31 Jan.	Shops in Ballydesmond burned as a reprisal.
1 Feb.	Cornelius Murphy, Rathmore, executed in Cork Jail.
4 Feb.	Bridget Walpole of Ballyea goes missing.
	Jer Galvin of Listowel dies after being forced to work on the roads.
5 Feb.	Body of Bridget Walpole found shot dead.
6 Feb.	Joseph Taylor of Glencar arrested by the RIC and later shot.
7 Feb.	Sergeant and RIC constable wounded by Auxiliaries in Tralee.
9 Feb.	Constable Molahy wounded in Abbeydorney.
10 Feb.	Eleven houses burned in Abbeydorney as a reprisal.

Horses seized around Tralee for cavalry search of the Dingle peninsula.

14 Feb.   Round-up in the Dingle peninsula begins.

19 Feb.   M. R. McElligott of Listowel killed.

21 Feb.   Young men in Dingle forced to work on the roads.

22 Feb.   Constables George H. Howlett and Wills shot dead in Ballylongford.

Constable Banks fired upon and an ambush aborted in Ballybunion.

Some twenty houses burned in Ballybunion as a reprisal.

24 Feb.   RIC boarding a train ambushed at Lisselton.

26 Feb.   Cycle party ambushed near Conor Pass by the IRA.

27 Feb.   Volunteer Joseph Taylor shot dead in custody in Glencar.

1 Mar.   General Strickland visits Tralee on tour of inspection.

Thomas Cotter shot outside his Carraclough home as a spy.

3 Mar.   Round-up of men in Tralee.

5 Mar.   Clonbanin Ambush; Brigadier General Hanway Cumming killed.

6 Mar.   Constable throws grenade after being assaulted in Tralee.

7 Mar.   James Kennelly of Lisselton shot dead by the RIC for 'refusing to stop'.

8 Mar.   Causeway RIC Barracks attacked. Three constables wounded.

9 Mar.   Head Constable of Killorglin escapes ambush outside his home.

12 Mar.   Cadet Walter Falkiner killed in train ambush near Tubrid.

13 Mar.   Seven-man RIC patrol ambushed in Killorglin, no injuries reported.

15 Mar.   Constable John Grant shot dead near Abbeydorney.

17 Mar.   Attack on RIC barracks in Farranfore.

21 Mar.   Train ambushed at Headford Junction. Volunteers Allman and Bailey killed.

Tans throw a small bomb on the street in Tralee, three civilians injured.

22 Mar.   Lispole Ambush. M. Fitzgerald of Minard and Thomas Hawley of Tralee killed.

23 Mar   T. M. Ashe of Lispole killed by British forces.

25 Mar.   Sardy O'Sullivan shot as a spy by the IRA near Kenmare.

26 Mar.   St John's parish church raked by gunfire in Tralee.

Volunteer Liam 'Sonny' McCarthy of Lixnaw killed in custody by Tans in Tralee.

2 Apr.   RIC barracks in Farranfore and Castleisland attacked.

6 Apr.   John 'Boxer' O'Mahony killed as a spy by the IRA in Tralee.

7 Apr.   Kilmorna Ambush, near Listowel. Volunteer Galvin killed.

12 Apr.   Daniel O'Driscoll, sixteen, shot dead and John O'Sullivan, fifteen, wounded by Auxiliaries at Liscahane, Ardfert.

14 Apr.	Sir Arthur Vicars killed by the IRA at Kilmorna.
15 Apr.	Major J. A. MacKinnon killed in Tralee assassination.
	Military ban hearings of criminal damage cases against crown forces.
	Twelve houses burned by Auxiliaries in Ballymacelligott.
15 Apr.	Volunteer John Reidy shot dead in Ballymacelligott by British forces.
19 Apr.	Tralee sacked by crown forces.
	RIC head constable of Castleisland ambushed on a train at Gortatlea.
21 Apr.	Denny O'Loughlin shot by the IRA in Tralee.
25 Apr.	Police patrol ambushed in Ardfert, no casualties.
26 Apr.	Military ambushed in Glenbeigh, three wounded.
27 Apr.	Four Listowel businesses destroyed by Black and Tans as a reprisal.
	Military announced reprisals to be taken against selected individuals in future.
30 Apr.	Patrick Molloy shot dead near Headford.
1 May	Denis Touchy, ex-RIC, killed after being arrested by the military in Kenmare.
4 May	Tom O'Sullivan shot as a spy by the IRA and his body used to lure the RIC and Black and Tans into an ambush at Bog Road, Rathmore. Eight constables are killed.
8 May	Head Constable William K. Storey and Sergeant Butler killed in Castleisland.
	Four constables ambushed in Farranfore, Constable Stockton wounded.
9 May	Three farmhouses burned in reprisal.
12 May	Volunteers Patrick Dalton, Jeremiah Lyons and Patrick Walsh killed at Knockanure.
14 May	Head Constable Francis Benson shot dead in Tralee.
	RIC patrol ambushed in Cahersiveen, one constable wounded.
15 May	Sergeant in Royal Fusiliers shot and wounded in Kenmare.
	All men rounded up in Cahersiveen.
16 May	Constable Kilgannon wounded in Cahersiveen Ambush.
17 May	District Inspector Frank Lancaster wounded in Ballymalis.
	Constable Charles F. Mead shot at Ballyseedy and buried in Ballyfinnane.
	Four businesses destroyed in Tralee as reprisal.
19 May	Volunteer T. O'Sullivan of Rathmore killed.
23 May	Large reinforcement of Auxiliaries and military arrive in Cahersiveen.
26 May	Volunteer John Sheehan shot dead four miles from Listowel by British forces.

27 May   Ballyheigue Castle burned by the IRA.

1 June   Five RIC killed in an ambush near Castlemaine, Volunteer Jerry Myles of Tralee wounded.

3 June   John 'Cousy' Fitzgerald kidnapped by the IRA in Tralee.

5 June   Fitzgerald shot as a spy at Ballybeggan, Tralee.

9 June   Train ambushed near Ballybrack, one soldier killed.

14 June   District Inspector Scully of Castleisland and three colleagues injured by Ballydwyer road mine.

Two Royal Marines injured in an ambush near Kenmare.

James Keane, retired RIC, shot as a spy by the IRA near Listowel.

22 June   Police convoy ambushed near Farranfore.

26 June   P. McCarthy killed in Killarney.

10 July   Eve of truce shootout in Castleisland, nine killed.

Two Black and Tans shot and wounded in Tarbert.

11 July   Two Royal Fusiliers shot in Killarney.

APPENDIX 4

Civil War timeline with special reference to Kerry

Compiled by Ryle Dwyer

1921

14–21 July President Éamon de Valera in London for talks with Prime Minister David Lloyd George.

11 Oct.   Anglo-Irish conference begins in London.

13 Nov.   Constables Sydney and Crittenden injured near Brosna.

6 Dec.   Anglo-Irish Treaty signed in London.

12 Dec.   Sergeant John Maher of County Carlow killed and Constable Gallagher wounded in Ballybunion.

14 Dec.   Treaty debate begins in Dáil.

19 Dec.   Austin Stack seconds de Valera's opposition to the Treaty.

23 Dec.   Dáil debate adjourned for Christmas.

26 Dec.   IRA reviewed by Austin Stack in Tralee.

1922

3 Jan.   Dáil debate resumes.

7 Jan.   Dáil approves the Treaty by 64–57 votes.

10 Jan.   De Valera defeated in presidential election.

11 Jan.   Arthur Griffith elected president.

20 Jan.   Percy Hannafin fatally wounded.

2 Feb.   Constable Charles F. Ednie killed in Killarney.

15 Mar.   De Valera launches new party, Cumann na Poblachta.

19 Mar.   De Valera holds rally in Killarney.

20 Mar.   De Valera holds rally in Tralee.

26 Mar.   Anti-Treaty IRA set up executive in Dublin.

7 Apr.   Unfounded reports of two RIC men killed and others wounded in Tralee.

13 Apr.   Republicans seize the Four Courts.

14 Apr.   De Valera says 'majority have no right to do wrong'.

22 Apr.	Michael Collins holds rally in Killarney.
23 Apr.	Collins holds rally in Tralee.
20 May	Collins and de Valera agree to election pact.
14 June	Collins appears to repudiate election pact.
16 June	Pro-Treaty candidates win overwhelming majority.
26 June	General J. J. O'Connell kidnapped by anti-Treaty IRA in the Four Courts.
28 June	National Army attacks the Four Courts.
30 June	IRA in the Four Courts surrender.
2 July	IRA Volunteer Thomas Flynn killed near Tralee.
5 July	Republican forces surrender in Dublin.
31 July	Members of the Dublin Guard embark for Kerry.
2 Aug.	Army lands at Fenit and seizes Tralee.
	IRA Volunteer John O'Sullivan killed at Kinfenora, near Fenit.
3 Aug.	Army lands at Tarbert and seizes Ballylongford and Listowel.
7 Aug.	Collins attends Mass for eleven Free State soldiers killed in fighting in Kerry.
11 Aug.	Army lands at Kenmare.
12 Aug.	Collins learns in Tralee of President Griffith's death.
22 Aug.	Collins killed at Béal na Bláth.
27 Aug.	Prisoner Seán Moriarty shot and left for dead by Free State troops in Tralee.
9 Sept.	IRA retake Kenmare, Tom Scarteen O'Connor killed.
24 Sept.	IRA attack on Killorglin.
10 Oct.	Catholic hierarchy denounces republican resistance.
15 Oct.	Emergency Powers granted to National Army by Dáil Éireann.
	Military courts set up.
	Unauthorised possession of firearms becomes a capital offence.
30 Oct.	John Lawlor's body found in Ballyheigue.
13 Nov.	Constable Albert Cruttenden of Kent injured in Brosna.
17 Nov.	Four IRA men executed in Dublin.
24 Nov.	Erskine Childers executed for possession of a gun.
30 Nov.	Three more IRA men executed in Dublin.
1 Dec.	IRA announces members of Dáil are liable to be shot.
6 Dec.	Irish Free State formally established.
8 Dec.	Volunteer William Harrington killed in Tralee.
19 Dec.	Four IRA men sentenced to death in Tralee.

1923

16 Jan.	Volunteer Eugene Fitzgerald killed in Free State custody at Ardfert.
20 Jan.	Four men executed in Tralee – James Daly, John Clifford, Michael Brosnan and James Hanlon.
23 Jan.	Volunteer Daniel Daly killed in Tralee.
20 Feb.	Stephen Fuller arrested in a dugout near Lixnaw.
6 Mar.	Five Free State soldiers killed by a trap mine in Knocknagoshel.
7 Mar.	Eight IRA prisoners killed at Ballyseedy – John Daly, Patrick Buckley, Patrick Hartnett, James Walsh, George O'Shea, T. Tuomey, T. O'Connor, Michael O'Connell.
	Four IRA prisoners killed at Countess Bridge, Killarney – Jeremiah O'Donoghue, Daniel O'Donoghue, Stephen Buckley, Tim Murphy.
8 Mar.	Volunteer James Taylor killed at Ballyseedy.
11 Mar.	Captain Frank O'Grady (IRA) killed after being taken prisoner in Killarney.
12 Mar.	Five IRA prisoners shot in the legs and then blown up near Cahersiveen. Jeremiah Casey of Beaufort killed in custody.
15 Mar.	Volunteer John Kevins killed in Beaufort.
21 Mar.	Army order to bury prisoners killed in custody.
22 Mar.	James Walsh of Currow arrested.
24 Mar.	De Valera proposes the IRA quit fighting.
27 Mar.	Body of James Walsh of Currow found by the roadside.
28 Mar.	Jack Fleming of Tralee arrested by Free State troops. His body is found the next day.
6 Apr.	Free State soldiers attack IRA billeted in Derry na Feena. George Nagle killed.
14 Apr.	Austin Stack captured.
18 Apr.	Timothy 'Aero' Lyons killed by Free State soldiers.
24 Apr.	Daniel Murphy killed in custody by Free State soldiers.
25 Apr.	Three IRA executed in Tralee: Edward Greaney, Reginald Hathaway and James McInerney.
27 Apr.	IRA ceasefire comes into effect at noon.
24 May	IRA ordered to dump arms.
29 May	Volunteer Jeremiah O'Leary killed in custody in Castleisland.

BIBLIOGRAPHY

Books:

Abbott, Richard, *Police Casualties in Ireland, 1919–1922* (Mercier Press, Cork, 2000)

Allen, Gregory, *The Garda Síochána: Policing Independent Ireland 1922–82* (Gill & Macmillan, Dublin, 1999)

Andrew, Christopher, *Secret Service: The Making of the British Intelligence Community* (Guild Publishing, London, 1985)

Barrett, J. J., *In the Name of the Game* (Private, Dublin, 1997)

Burke, Marcus, *The O'Rahilly* (Anvil Books, Tralee, 1967)

Carroll, Aideen, *Seán Moylan: Rebel Leader* (Mercier Press, Cork, 2010)

Casement, Roger, *The Crime Against Europe: Writings and Poems of Roger Casement*, edited by Herbert O. Mackey (C. J. Fallon, Dublin, 1966)

Casement, Roger, *One Bold Deed of Open Treason: The Berlin Diary of Roger Casement, 1914–1916*, edited by Angus Mitchell (Merrion Press, Dublin, 2016)

Caulfield, Max, *The Easter Rebellion* (2nd edn, Gill & Macmillan, Dublin, 1995)

Comyn, James, *Irish at Law: A Selection of Famous and Unusual Cases* (Martin Secker & Warburg, London, 1981)

Cronin, Seán, *The McGarrity Papers* (Anvil Books, Tralee, 1972)

Deasy, Liam, *Towards Ireland Free* (Mercier Press, Cork, 1973)

Deasy, Liam, *Brother Against Brother* (Mercier Press, Cork, 1982)

Doyle, Tom, *The Civil War in Kerry* (Mercier Press, Cork, 2008)

Dudley Edwards, Ruth, *Patrick Pearse: The Triumph of Failure* (Irish Academic Press, Dublin, 2006)

Dwyer, T. Ryle, *Big Fellow, Long Fellow: A Joint Biography of Collins and De Valera* (Gill & Macmillan, Dublin, 1998)

Dwyer, T. Ryle, *The Squad* (Mercier Press, Cork, 2005)

Dwyer, T. Ryle, *'I Signed My Death Warrant': Michael Collins & The Treaty* (Mercier Press, Cork, 2006)

Dwyer, T. Ryle, *Michael Collins: The Man Who Won the War* (rev. edn, Mercier Press, Cork, 2009)

Dwyer, T. Ryle, *Michael Collins and the Civil War* (Mercier Press, Cork, 2012)

Fitzpatrick, David, *Politics and Irish Life 1913–1921: Provincial Experience of War and Revolution* (Cork University Press, Cork, 1998)

Gaughan, J. Anthony, *A Political Odyssey: Thomas O'Donnell (M.P. for West Kerry 1900–1918)* (Kingdom Books, Dublin, 1983)

Gaughan, J. Anthony, *Listowel and Its Vicinity* (Kingdom Books, Dublin, 1973)

Gaughan, J. Anthony, *Austin Stack: Portrait of a Separatist* (Kingdom Books, Dublin, 1977)

Gaughan, J. Anthony, *The Memoirs of Constable Jeremiah Mee, RIC* (Mercier Press, Cork, 2012)

Griffith, Kenneth, *Curious Journey* (Mercier Press, Cork, 1973)

Gwynn, Denis, *Traitor or Patriot? The Life and Death of Roger Casement* (J. Cape & H. Smith, New York, 1931)

Harrington, Niall C., *Kerry Landing* (Anvil Books, Dublin, 1992)

Herlihy, Jim, *The Royal Irish Constabulary: A Short History and Genealogical Guide* (Four Courts Press, Dublin, 1997)

Hopkinson, Michael, *Green against Green: The Irish Civil War* (Gill & Macmillan, Dublin, 1988)

Horgan, Tim, *Dying for the Cause: Kerry's Republican Dead* (Mercier Press, Cork, 2015)

Hyde, H. Montgomery, *Famous Trials 9: Roger Casement* (Penguin Books, London, 1964)

Inglis, Brian, *Roger Casement* (Hodder and Stoughton, London, 1973)

Joy, Sinéad, *The IRA in Kerry 1916–1921* (The Collins Press, Cork, 2005)

Kerryman, The, *Kerry's Fighting Story 1916–1921* (The Kerryman, Tralee, 1947)

Kerryman, The, *With the IRA in the Fight for Freedom* (The Kerryman, Tralee, 1952)

Kerryman, The, *Sworn to be Free: The Complete Book of IRA Jailbreaks 1918–1921* (Anvil Books, Tralee, 1971)

Kissane, Bill, *The Politics of the Irish Civil War* (Oxford University Press, Oxford, 2005)

Knott, George H., *The Trial of Roger Casement (1917)* (Kessinger Publishing, Montana, 2007)

Lynch, Florence Monteith, *The Mystery Man of Banna Strand: Irish Brigade 1915–16* (Vantage Press, New York, 1959)

Macardle, Dorothy, *Tragedies of Kerry* (Emton Press, Dublin, 1924)

Macardle, Dorothy, *The Irish Republic: A Documented Chronicle of the Anglo-Irish Conflict and the Partitioning of Ireland with a Detailed Account of the Period 1916–23* (Corgi, London, 1968)

MacColl, René, *Roger Casement* (Hamish Hamilton, London, 1956)

MacEoin, Uinseann, *Survivors: The Story of Ireland's Struggle as Told through Some of Her*

Outstanding Living People Recalling Events from the Days of Davitt, through James Connolly, Brugha, Collins, Liam Mellows, and Rory O'Connor, to the Present Time (Argenta Publications, Dublin, 1980)

Martin, Thomas F., *The Kingdom in the Empire: Kerry in World War One* (Nonsuch Publishing, Dublin, 2006)

McAuliffe, Bridget, McAuliffe, Mary and O'Shea, Owen, *Kerry 1916: Histories and Legacies of the Easter Rising* (Irish Historical Publications, Kerry, 2016)

McGarry, Fearghal, *The Rising, Ireland: Easter 1916* (Oxford University Press, Oxford, 2010)

Moore, Martin, *The Call to Arms: Tom McEllistrim and the Fight for Freedom in Kerry* (Private, Tralee, 2016)

Mulcahy, Risteárd, *My Father, the General: Richard Mulcahy and the Military History of the Revolution* (Liberties Press, Dublin, 2009)

Murphy, Donie, *'The Men of The South' in the War of Independence* (Inch Publications, Midleton, 1991)

Murphy, Jeremiah, *When Youth Was Mine: A Memoir of Kerry 1902–1925* (Mentor Press, Dublin, 1998)

Neeson, Eoin, *The Civil War in Ireland 1922–23* (Mercier Press, Cork, 1966)

O'Brien Paul, *Field of Fire: The Battle of Ashbourne, 1916* (New Island, Dublin, 2012)

O'Connor, Seamus, *Tomorrow Was Another Day* (Anvil Books, Tralee, 1970)

O'Donoghue, Florence, *No Other Law* (Anvil Books, Dublin, 1986)

O'Farrell, Padraic, *Who's Who in the Irish War of Independence and Civil War 1916–1923* (Lilliput Press, Dublin, 1997)

O'Keeffe, Hélène, *To Speak of Easter Week* (Mercier Press, Cork, 2015)

Ó Luing, Seán, *'I Die in a Good Cause'* (Anvil Books, Tralee, 1970)

O'Mahony, Seán, *Frongoch: University of Revolution* (FDR Teoranta, Dublin, 1987)

O'Malley, Ernie, *The Singing Flame* (Anvil Books, Dublin, 1978)

O'Malley, Ernie, *The Men Will Talk to Me: Kerry Interviews*, edited by Cormac O'Malley and Tim Horgan (Mercier Press, Cork, 2012)

O'Sullivan, Donal J., *The Irish Constabularies 1822–1922: A Century of Policing in Ireland* (Brandon Books, Dingle, 1999)

O'Sullivan, Donal J., *District Inspector John A. Kearney* (Trafford Publishing, Bloomington, 2005)

Pearse, P. H., *Ghosts: Tracts for the Times* (Whelan, Dublin, 1916)

Regan, John M., *The Irish Counter Revolution 1921–1936* (Gill & Macmillan, Dublin, 1991)

Ryan, Meda, *The Real Chief: The Story of Liam Lynch* (Mercier Press, Cork, 1986)

Spindler, Captain Karl, *The Mystery of the Casement Ship* (Anvil Books, Tralee, 1965)

Townshend, Charles, *The British Campaign in Ireland 1919–1921* (Oxford University Press, Oxford, 1975)

Yeats, W. B., *Collected Poems: Yeats* (Picador, London, 2003)

Younger, Calton, *Ireland's Civil War* (Frederick Muller, London, 1968)

Articles:

Daly, Denny, 'The Ballykissane Pier Tragedy of 1916: 34 Years Afterwards. Denny Daly Tells His Story,' *The Kerryman*, 29 July 1950

Dee, Con, 'The Valley of Knockanure,' *Shannonside Annual* (1958), pp. 13–30

FitzGerald, Desmond, 'Inside the GPO', *The Irish Times*, 7 April 1966

Kennan, Austin, 'Ballyduff Man's Part in the 1916 Rising', *The Kerryman*, 19 November 1966

Lynch, Denis, 'The Years of Ambushes and Round-Ups,' *Journal of Cumann Luachra,* Vol. 1, No. 5 (June 1989), pp. 54–57

McDiarmid, Lucy, 'Secular Relics: Casement's Boat, Casement's Dish' http://www.tandfonline.com/doi/abs/10.1080/095023602761622351?journalCode=rtpr20

Moynihan, Manus, 'Troubled Times: A First Hand Account of the Bog Road Ambush,' *Journal of Cumann Luachra*, Vol. 1, No. 1 (1982), pp. 15–19

Ó Ceilleachair, Seán, 'Tureengarrive Ambush,' *Journal of Cumann Luachra*, Vol. 1, No. 2 (1983), pp. 44–51

Spillane, Denis, 'Rathmore: E Company, 5th Battalion: Kerry No. 2 Brigade,' *Journal of Cumann Luachra*, Vol. 1, No. 2 (1983), pp. 40–41

Stack, Austin, 'Thomas Aghás: The Story of a Noble Life and Heroic Death', *The Kerry Champion,* 29 September 1928

Stack, Austin, 'The Landing of Casement', *The Kerry Champion*, 7 September 1929

Waters, John, 'Children of the Rising', *The Irish Times*, 4 April 1991

Newspapers:

Irish Independent

Irish Times, The

Kerry Advocate

Kerry Champion, The

Kerry Evening Post
Kerry People, The
Kerry Sentinel
Kerry Weekly Reporter, The
Kerryman, The
Killarney Echo, The
Liberator (Tralee), The

Bureau of Military History Witness Statements
(www.bureauofmilitaryhistory.ie)

Aoife de Burca, WS 359

Charles Saurin, WS 288

Daniel Dennehy, WS 116

Éamonn T. Dore, WS 153

Feargus de Burca, WS 694

Fionán Lynch, WS 192

Harry Colley, WS 1687

Jerry Golden, WS 177

Joseph Lawless, WS 1043

Kevin O'Sheil, WS 1770

Mary Josephine Mulcahy (Ryan), WS 399

Maurice Moriarty, WS 117

Michael Knightly, WS 833

Michael McAllister, WS 1494

Michael W. O'Reilly, WS 886

Nora Ashe, WS 645

Paddy Paul Fitzgerald, WS 1079

Richard Hayes, WS 97

Richard Mulcahy, WS 399

Tadhg Kennedy, WS 1413

Thomas McEllistrim, WS 882

Una C. Stack, WS 214

THE CONTRIBUTORS

Simon Brouder is the senior news reporter at *The Kerryman* and has worked at the paper since 2004. He holds an MA in modern Irish history from University College Cork and an MA in journalism from NUI Galway. He is also a regular contributor to various national titles.

T. Ryle Dwyer was born in the United States and reared from the age of four in Tralee, where he received all his primary and secondary education. He has a doctorate in history from the University of North Texas, and is the author of over twenty books on different aspects of Irish history. These include *Tans, Terror and Troubles*, on the War of Independence and Civil War in Kerry, and *Big Fellow, Long Fellow*, a joint biography of Éamon de Valera and Michael Collins. He is also the author of a biography on Éamon de Valera in the *Irish Independent*'s Great Biography series, as well as *The Squad* and a trilogy of books on the life of Michael Collins – *The Man Who Won the War, I Signed My Death Warrant* and *Michael Collins and the Civil War*, all published by Mercier Press.

Tralee native **Dónal Nolan** is deputy editor of *The Kerryman*, where he has worked for the past twelve years. He comes from a family steeped in the newspaper, being a great-grandson of one of the founders of *The Kerryman*, Daniel Nolan. Dónal is a graduate of Gaelcholáiste Chiarraí in his hometown and of NUI Galway. He is also the author of *The Kerry Way: A Walking Guide*.

Brian Ó Conchubhair, a native of Oakpark in Tralee, is associate professor of Irish language and literature and a fellow of the Keough-Naughton Institute for Irish Studies at the University of Notre Dame. He has been a visiting professor at Université Sorbonne Nouvelle in Paris and Charles University in Prague. His publications include *Fin de Siècle na Gaeilge: Darwin, An Athbheochan agus Smaointeoireacht na hEorpa*, a monograph on the intellectual history of the Irish revival.

Hélène O'Keeffe is a Cork-based historian with a research focus on twentieth-century Irish history, commemoration, memory and oral tradition. Originally from Tralee, she studied history in University College Cork and was awarded a doctorate in modern Irish history in 2009. She taught English and history at secondary level for fifteen years, and from 2015 has worked as a researcher on the *Atlas of the Irish Revolution* (forthcoming, Cork University Press). Her book *To Speak of Easter Week: Family Memories of the Irish Revolution*, based on research funded by the Department of Arts, Heritage and the Gaeltacht, was published by Mercier Press in October 2015. She is currently working as a post-doctorate research fellow in University College Cork.

INDEX

MERCIER PRESS

IRISH PUBLISHER - IRISH STORY

We hope you enjoyed this book.

Since 1944, Mercier Press has published books that have been critically important to Irish life and culture. Books that dealt with subjects that informed readers about Irish scholars, Irish writers, Irish history and Ireland's rich heritage.

We believe in the importance of providing accessible histories and cultural books for all readers and all who are interested in Irish cultural life.

Our website is the best place to find out more information about Mercier, our books, authors, news and the best deals on a wide variety of books. Mercier tracks the best prices for our books online and we seek to offer the best value to our customers, offering free delivery within Ireland.

Sign up on our website to receive updates and special offers.

www.mercierpress.ie
www.facebook.com/mercier.press
www.twitter.com/irishpublisher

Mercier Press, Unit 3b, Oak House, Bessboro Rd, Blackrock, Cork, Ireland